"Beware of all enterprises that require new clothes."

HENRY DAVID THOREAU, *Walden*

CHIC
SIMPLE ®

C L O T H E S

THAMES AND HUDSON

FIRST PUBLISHED IN GREAT BRITIAN IN 1993
BY THAMES AND HUDSON LTD. LONDON
REPRINTED 1994, 1995, 1996

KIM JOHNSON GROSS   JEFF STONE
WRITTEN BY CHRISTA WORTHINGTON
PHOTOGRAPHS BY JAMES WOJCIK
ILLUSTRATIONS BY ERIC HANSON

MENSWEAR EDITOR: JOHN MATHER
WOMENSWEAR EDITOR: AMANDA MANOGUE BURCH
SPORTSWEAR EDITOR: HOLLY HILLENBRAND

DESIGN AND ART DIRECTION BY GROUP INCORPORATED

Printed and bound in Britain
by Butler and Tanner Ltd, Frome and London

WITH LOVE TO MY MOTHER, EVELYN JOHNSON,
FOR TEACHING ME CHIC SIMPLE,
AND TO MRS. ETIENNE BOEGNER, FOR HER FRIENDSHIP
K.J.G.

TO JANE—MY RODEO QUEEN
J.S.

FOR TOPPY AND GLORIA
C.W.

"The more you know, the less you need."

AUSTRALIAN ABORIGINAL
SAYING

CONTENTS

13   FOUNDATION
Design Context: A history of fashion as a cultural manifestation from the 1930s to the present

25   BASICS
Survival Gear: A blueprint of clothing essentials from underwear to formalwear

67   STYLE
Elements of Style: A primer to fabric, tailoring, and value

79   OPTIONS
Personal Style: Accessories and clothes that broaden a basic wardrobe

1 0 9   **A C T I V E**
All Sport: From land to sea, a look at the most up-to-date in fabric, construction, and style in clothes for sports

1 4 3   **M I X I N G**
Versatility: Adapting the most basic wardrobe to any occasion by combining the unexpected

1 6 1   **F A M I L Y**
Toddler to Teen: Finding clothes that fit children's mental and physical ages, while meeting the needs of parents

1 7 5   **W H E R E**
Worldwide retail guide: Chic Simple clothes as sold through retailers, outlets, and catalogues

CHIC
SIMPLE

Chic Simple is a primer for living well but sensibly in the 1990s. It's for those who believe that quality of life does not come in accumulating things, but in paring down to the essentials, with a commitment to home, community, and the environment. In a world of limited resources, Chic Simple enables readers to bring value and style into their lives with economy and simplicity.

FOUNDATION

From the cycles of trends, classics evolve. Classics transcend a particular place or decade. They are about style that endures because it works. ✎ In the presumed frivolity of fashion, there is engineering as influential as the Roman aqueduct. Clothes are affected by industry and commerce, by science and psychology. Clothing tells the truth about an age without the advantage of hindsight. ✎ The progress of sartorial development has been a continual reshuffling of tried and true forms until rules of dress have been adjusted beyond recognition. ✎ To understand the present, it's helpful to look at the past.

NINETEEN 30s

EVENTS

The Stock Market Crash, 1929. The New Deal, 1932. Aldous Huxley publishes *Brave New World*, 1932. *Kristallnacht* in Germany, 1938

PEOPLE

Cole Porter, Al Capone, Clark Gable, Marlene Dietrich, Greta Garbo, Benito Mussolini, Fred Astaire, Raymond Hood, Pablo Picasso, Franklin D. Roosevelt, the Duke of Windsor and Wallis Simpson, Le Corbusier

FASHION NEWS

Sportswear. Pants for women. Knits. The bias cut and cowl collar. Nylon stockings

FASHION CAPITALS

Hollywood, Paris

DESIGNERS

Coco Chanel, Madeleine Vionnet, Edward Molyneux, Edith Head

THE DECADE OF BIG BAND

SOUND, BIG SCREEN GLAMOUR, AND BUSBY BERKELEY SPECTACLE PROVIDED

DISTRACTION FROM GRIM REALITIES: ECONOMIC DEPRESSION AND THE

rise of Hitler. On celluloid, life was all top hats, tap dances, and feather boas. Real life was about soup kitchens

and unemployment lines. From realism—painted by Edward Hopper and Grant Wood—came the Modernism

of the mechanized age. Form followed function with graphic black-and-white clarity. Industrial design replaced

Art Deco. Aerodynamic curves appeared on cars, buildings, appliances, and airplanes; life accelerated

and sportswear became part of everyday attire. Women took to wide-legged pants, and to the mannish cardigan

sweaters that Coco Chanel borrowed from the English gentleman. Lana Turner popularized knits and twin-

set sweaters. Backs plunged on dresses and bathing suits, the latter finally used as much for swimming

as sunbathing. Clothes relaxed, but with elegance. In Paris, Madeleine Vionnet engineered the bias cut

and cowl collar—a freed-up silhouette that achieved Hellenic simplicity. Hollywood was glamour's

vehicle, while hand-me-downs and sturdy suits, bought by mail-order catalogue, were the garb of real life.

Cary Grant in a double-breasted suit, or Katharine Hepburn in trousers, model elegance to this day.

NINETEEN

40s

WORLD WAR II CAST A PALL OF AUSTERITY, AS THE RATIONING OF ALL VALUABLE

materials—including cloth—dictated silhouette: men's vests and pant cuffs were abandoned; women wore skinny skirts and even cork-platformed shoes, popularized by Carmen Miranda, saved leather. By war's end, America was buoyed by expectations of prosperity and an influx

EVENTS

Pearl Harbor, 1941. The end of World War II, 1945. The Nuremberg trials, 1946. George Orwell's *1984* is published in 1949.

PEOPLE

Harry Truman, General Patton, Judy Garland, Cary Grant, Betty Grable, Winston Churchill, Arshile Gorky, Tennessee Williams, Orson Welles, Raymond Chandler, Frank Sinatra, Mies van der Rohe

FASHION NEWS

The New Look. The Zoot suit. Rolled-up blue jeans. The Eisenhower jacket

FASHION CAPITALS

New York during the war, then Paris

DESIGNERS

Christian Dior

of European talent in all areas of the arts. Norman Norell and Charles James from England and Pauline Trigère from Paris set up shop in New York. With Paris under siege, American designers could shine: Adrian and Mainbocher made fashion with whatever was at hand. But in 1947, Christian Dior's "New Look"— a full, curvy silhouette—ushered in a fresh spate of elegant French couture. Tribal teen culture emerged complete with slang, rolled-up jeans, bobby socks, and "hepcat" Zoot suits. Hollywood played out paradigms of masculine elegance from the rugged to the refined: Bogart's trench coat and Cary Grant's black tie.

IN AMERICA, IT WAS THE AGE OF CON-
SUMER POWER, CORPORATE
conformity, and the suburban nuclear
family. Everything—from hair to fur-
niture—took its modern sculptural
form. While Europe remained hobbled
by postwar reconstruction, America
flexed its muscles. It tested atomic
bombs in the desert, patrolled Korea,
produced labor-saving appliances for
the home, and blacklisted accused
Communists in Hollywood. Design
reflected energy, optimism, and kitsch
with kidney-shaped tables, tail-finned
Cadillacs, and frenetic patterns on
curtains, wallpaper, plastics, and
Formica. Youth codified its own style
with rock 'n' roll and split ranks between
Elvis-coiffed rebels and the Ivy League.
The cinema created heroes out of brood-
ing bad boys. James Dean (in *Rebel
Without a Cause*, 1955) and Marlon
Brando (*The Wild One*, 1951) made jeans,
T-shirts, and motorcycle jackets a cult.
America finally had its own fashion:
Claire McCardell's "American Look."
Her practical separates, flat shoes, and

AEVENTS

The McCarthy trials. A
million television
viewers watch A-bomb
testing in Nevada in
1952. The Korean
War and the Cold
War. Buckminster
Fuller's Geodesic
Dome house, 1952

PEOPLE

Dwight D.
Eisenhower, Elvis
Presley, Albert Camus,
Marilyn Monroe, Joe
DiMaggio, Jackson
Pollock, Montgomery
Clift, Gordon
Bunshaft, Alvar Aalto

FASHION NEWS

The American Look—
casual separates.
Motorcycle jackets.
Capri pants. Flats. The
sheath. The Little
Black Dress. Plaid.
Headbands. Pedal
pushers

FASHION CAPITALS

Paris, New York

DESIGNERS

Claire McCardell,
Balenciaga,
Charles James

wrap-around dresses in plain fabrics sold
across the country through the Fuller
Brush catalogue. Glamour in this decade
acquired a contrived yet naive sensuality
in the sheath dresses of Marilyn Monroe
and Brigitte Bardot. Paris couture voiced
a protest against mass production with
displays of hand-sewn splendor. Cristobal
Balenciaga's clothes swooped and
curved in architectural A-lines, zigzags,
and ovals; in New York, couturier
Charles James dressed society in yards of
celadon satin. By decade's end, a young
Yves Saint Laurent, heir to the late
Christian Dior, gave the first suggestion
that even couture would take its cue
from the street, with a youthful collection of knits and leather jackets.

NINETEEN 50s

The decade of revolution broke with tradition to create new icons of modernity—the miniskirt, Star Trek tunics, bodysuits, and Vidal Sassoon haircuts—only to assault them with the counterculture uniform of blue jeans, T-shirts, and long, unkempt hair. It was the era that launched unisex and ready-to-wear, and dethroned the stylistic supremacy of Paris couture. The pedestrian and the commonplace had new stature; Campbell's soup cans became art. Pop culture popped, via television—by 1960, 85 million TV sets were installed in America, with another 10.5 million in Britain—and clothes came under the spell of the music industry. Fashion was democratized. Abbie Hoffman, the Yippie dissident, wore a shirt made of the Stars and Stripes on American television and was arrested for desecrating the flag. The medium was the message. Half the U.S. population was under twenty-five. All ears, even those of haute couture designers, were to the ground, listening for the youthful step of a new streetwise muse: an androgynous Twiggy. Faith in technology and the future—evident in the vinyls and see-through plastics of Pierre Cardin, and André Courrèges, or the Mod style of Mary Quant—crumbled with the end of Camelot. Clothes retreated to the garden of hippiedom and became body art, manifestations of the soul. Fashion's mandate was forever subverted: Everyone in the Western world wore jeans, but in a manner unique to him or her. The uniform of the individual had arrived.

nineteen sixties

EVENTS The Kennedy assassinations, 1963 (JFK) and 1968 (RFK). The civil rights movement. Race riots in Watts, 1965. Woodstock, 1968. First man on the moon, 1969 **PEOPLE** The Beatles, Martin Luther King, Jacqueline Kennedy, Jimi Hendrix, Twiggy, Roy Lichtenstein, Jean Shrimpton, Christine Keeler, Jane Fonda, Bob Dylan, Joan Baez, Cesar Chavez, Paolo Soleri **FASHION NEWS** Street fashion. The advent of ready-to-wear. The mini. Mod. Catsuits. Blue jeans. T-shirts with a message. Long hair **FASHION CAPITALS** London, Paris **DESIGNERS** Mary Quant, Pierre Cardin, André Courrèges, Yves Saint Laurent, Zandra Rhodes, Levi Strauss, Emilio Pucci

nineteen seventies

This was the decade of doubt and diminished expectations: the oil crisis, Watergate, and the aftershock of the Sixties could not be entirely danced away at the disco. Fashion seemed to be giving out mixed messages. The nylon shirts and polyester suits of *Saturday Night Fever* were forward-looking by virtue of fiber, but their flared bell-bottoms and wide lapels were romantic, foppish, nostalgic. Cynicism and lack of faith in the future stalled style between the high-tech and handcrafted, leading inexorably toward Punk. Much of peasant/exotic hippie fashion found its way into mass-market ready-to-wear design in the Seventies. Yves Saint Laurent and Kenzo, a new talent from Japan, set the tone in Paris with bohemian, gypsy, and ethnic looks. Sportswear went out at night in the form of T-shirts and sweatshirts, now used by designers as evening wear. Interest in physical fitness made tracksuits and leotards part of the everyday wardrobe. High schools across America gave up on dress codes, and women wore pants to the office.

As informality gained ground, fashion found a new hierarchy—status dressing—by which even the humble blue jean could acquire "designer" cachet. Designers themselves became celebrities, and their names proliferated on towels, sheets, sunglasses, luggage, and cosmetics. American and Italian design became more influential. Giorgio Armani, a menswear designer, led the Milanese into prominence with deconstructed pantsuits for women. Ralph Lauren, formerly a tie salesman, had begun to think big—beyond items—to market total environments.

EVENTS Watergate. The oil crisis **PEOPLE** Richard Nixon, Jimmy Carter, Cheryl Tiegs, Renee Richards, Andy Warhol, John Travolta, Bjorn Borg, Mother Teresa, Brooke Shields, John Belushi, Mick and Bianca Jagger, Liza Minnelli, Henry Kissinger, Woodward and Bernstein, Terence Conran, I. M. Pei, Charles Moore, Robert Venturi **FASHION NEWS** Knits. Designer and novelty jeans. Bell-bottoms. The midi. Hot pants. Polyester pantsuits. T-shirt and sweatshirt dressing. Logoed T-shirts. Tracksuits. Shawls. Punk. Streaking **FASHION CAPITALS** Paris, Milan, New York, Tokyo **DESIGNERS** Kenzo, Yves Saint Laurent, Calvin Klein, Norma Kamali, Giorgio Armani, Betsey Johnson, Halston, Stephen Burrows

In the eighties of

Reagan and Thatcher, life imitated soap

opera. With Princess Diana, Madonna, and

Donald Trump, "Dynasty" seemed just like

real life and clothes emoted conservatism,

power, and wealth. For the first time since

blue jeans stormed the barricades of

formality, couture fashion became vital. Karl

Lagerfeld reinvented Chanel's traditional

tweed suits for the MTV generation. You

were what you wore—the wide shoulders of

the Armani power suit threw their weight

around Wall Street; status symbols stamped

Fendi or Cartier were counterfeited around

the globe; and designers became CEOs of

EVENTS

Reaganomics. AIDS identified, 1981. Black Monday, 1987. Iran-contra. Perestroika. Fall of the Berlin Wall, 1989

PEOPLE

Margaret Thatcher, Vaclav Havel, Arnold Schwarzenegger, Julian Schnabel, Mikhail Gorbachev, Oliver North, Pope John Paul II, Rock Hudson, Michael Graves

NINETEEN

80s

FASHION NEWS

Couture revival. Status dressing. Pearls. The pouf skirt. The Gap

DESIGNERS

Karl Lagerfeld, Giorgio Armani, Azzedine Alaïa, Yohji Yamamoto, Jean-Paul Gaultier, Donna Karan, Ralph Lauren

FASHION CAPITALS

Paris, Milan, New York, Tokyo, Barcelona

multinational corporations. Technology

brought not only the fax and the VCR but

advances such as heat-molded, rubberized

knits and seams. With them, even the most

casual sportswear took an S curve. Comfort

could be glamorized: bicycle shorts showed

a new urbanity and microfiber could wash

and wear, breathe, and still drape like

crepe. Stylistic conceits, from faux sur-

faces to nouvelle cuisine, eventually

triggered a craving for authenticity. By

mid-decade, sales of Levi's original jean,

the 501, had climbed, and the high-tech

outdoor clothing of Patagonia had become,

without benefit of advertising, a cult.

NINETEEN 90s

IF HISTORY IS THE JUDGE, CEN-TURIES CONCLUDE CREATIVELY, DESPITE ALL THE PRESSURES UPON them. Already, eco-friendly fashion has emerged in deed not just gesture with naturally colored cotton that eliminates the toxic dying process altogether. How design will manifest the decade's challenges is not yet apparent. But the demands on it are laid out: it must have a built-in rationale, as clear as a Le Corbusier blueprint. It has to perform with integrity and purpose, as well as please the eye. Values have shifted. Gross consumption no longer makes sense in the face of shrinking natural resources. Technology seems to have invaded spare time, not expanded it. With the mind cluttered, the body wants relief and a streamlining of stimuli. There's a new demand for comfort. To "live well" today requires paring down paraphernalia—simplification. The ideal is to travel light through life with a suitcase of essentials: real clothes.

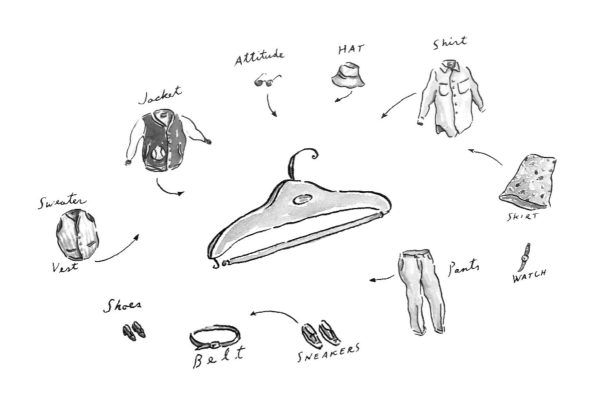

BASICS

- [ ] Underwear
- [ ] Socks
- [ ] Shoes
- [ ] T-shirt
- [ ] Shirt
- [ ] Turtleneck
- [ ] Polo shirt
- [ ] Jeans
- [ ] Slacks
- [ ] Khakis
- [ ] Blazer
- [ ] Suit
- [ ] Formalwear
- [ ] Trench coat

Simplify. ✎ A wardrobe needs to be built upon a few basics—the pants, jackets, shirts, and skirts you need to get by. Begin with a sense of purpose, a plan. Ask "where" and "when" before "what to wear?" Next, chart a color scheme to get the most flexibility from a limited number of clothes: choose a neutral shade of black, gray, navy, or beige as a base. ✎ The more costly the purchase, the more useful and versatile a garment should be. Wild prints and colors are best reserved for accent pieces. Think of packing a suitcase for a long trip and how much more pleasant it is to travel light.

Men's Underwear.

Boxer shorts are as emblematic of manhood as attire can be. Perhaps because of this iconic quality, women tend to prefer them to briefs. Young coeds in the mid-Eighties created a fad for cross-dressing with boxers, wearing them as loungewear or over leggings. With that, shorts lost the old-fogey stigma that had settled over them since the Sixties and began to recover a younger customer. Tastes in men's underwear have diversified in recent years, with briefs sharing drawer space with boxers, in a range of color and pattern. In the Eighties, boxers in novelty prints were worn as shorts and beachwear. Body-conscious streamlining has shrunk underwear generally, down to the skimpy extreme of the bikini thong. In boxers, waists have dropped slightly and legs are often slit—most unlike what grandfather would have worn.

BOXERS

They took their name when heavyweight fighters Jim Corbett and Bob Fitzsimmons abandoned traditional boxers' tights for trunks.

Winston Churchill liked to wear pale pink silk underwear.

JOCKEY BRIEFS

They were launched in 1934 after a company executive took inspiration from men wearing bikinis on the Riviera.

Sperm count and motility can be diminished by raised body temperature. If fertility is a concern, tight-fitting briefs and clothing are not advised during and after workouts.

BRA

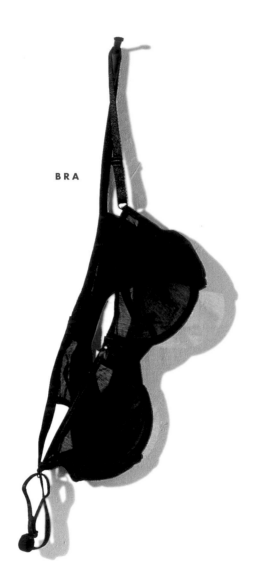

BUSTIER

L i n g e r i e . Black underwear is not just an indulgence; it can, in the right circumstance, function as outerwear—or underwear that shows. Madonna's way of wearing bustiers and lace with blue jeans exposed lingerie as a fashion influence, felt through the Eighties in increased transparency in clothes and a sportier use of lace. Lingerie also feeds cravings for a private experience of luxury— the sensation of satin on skin—as the success of the Victoria's Secret mail-order catalogue attests. Basic

CAMISOLE

CONTROL PANTY

black lends itself to exposure: The camisole can be worn as a top in the evening, and the bustier can reveal itself, more or less, depending on construction. Aerobic clothing has also raised the visibility of underwear with midriff, or bra, athletic tops and thongs. Sculpted underwear still serves its old purpose of contouring the body, but it does so with much greater comfort. The control panty improves on the girdle by ironing out bulges with uniform elasticity.

SOCKS

PROVIDE MEN WITH AN OPPORTUNITY FOR SELF-EXPRESSION. David Hockney, the painter, usually wears a different color sock on each foot. Amid all the personalizing possibilities, the dark sock provides an essential service of simplification. It maintains a monochromatic line with dark business suits, and avoids having to make a "statement" at all. Similarly, the sheer dark stocking is versatile for women. It can travel well from the office to the evening.

Sock Etiquette. Rules of attire are strangely precise about this region of the body. Skin must never be exposed between trouser cuff and sock. Casual clothes take thick socks in ribbed wool or argyle knit. Business clothes are worn with thin socks in smooth or ribbed cotton, and formal clothing requires silk stockings. Woolen socks can be worn on city streets, but dress socks clash with casual clothes. The most irreverent sock etiquette is not to wear them at all with loafers or moccasins, in the manner of preppies and Miami cops.

THE ARGYLE, originally worn with Scottish kilts, launched an explosion of color in men's hosiery in the Seventies.

NYLON MICROFIBER

Blended with Lycra, microfiber has made stockings fit and feel better than ever. The fineness of the fiber makes them cling and feel as soft as silk, even though they are run-resistant and long lasting. Flesh-colored stockings first appeared in 1922 and were improved upon by nylons, patented in 1937. In the Sixties, thick dancers' tights were made in thinner weaves to become "pantyhose" worn under minis.

"First, I'd put money into shoes.
No variety, just something I could
wear with everything . . ."

DIANA VREELAND

34

BLACK SHOES

ARE FORMAL BY VIRTUE OF COLOR, AND WORK WITH evening as well as business clothes. For men, the black cap-toe shoe is the dressiest business shoe one can own: it automatically adheres to the rule that business shoes must never be a shade lighter than suits. The cap-toe comes plain or with a medallion decoration and is worn with suits of worsted or flannel. The advantage of the black pump for women is that it looks businesslike as well as elegant. Heel shape determines longevity: it's the fashion element that dates a shoe.

Casual Shoes. More than any other item, shoes define the degree of formality in clothing. Business shoes will always look peculiar with jeans. Brown shoes are inherently sporty and, in classic styles, work very well with casual clothes. Shoes should blend with attire through color, texture, and shape; chunkier English-style shoes are better matched to English and American-cut clothes than delicate Italian loafers. **The penny loafer,** which came from Norway in the Forties, is more relaxed, by a shade, than the tassel loafer, and frees one from laces. The suede oxford with a rubberized sole is a sturdier walking shoe that can,

"Wanna know if a guy is

FAMOUS SHOES
Dorothy's ruby slippers
Elvis Presley's blue suede shoes
Cinderella's glass slipper
Nikita Khrushchev's podium-pounding shoe
Mercury's winged sandals
Nancy Sinatra's boots
The Old Woman and the Shoe
Louis XIV's heels
Imelda Marcos's shoes

in modern adaptations, provide a lot of weather resistance through Vibram soles and silicone-injected leather uppers. **Suede,** as the Duke of Windsor discovered, is a more subtle and versatile material than leather. The Duke took it out of its strictly rural context and, by example, set a style in America for wearing brown shoes with blue suits, which his fellow Englishmen still resist.

SIGNS OF QUALITY: Heels made of layered leather, sometimes with a rubber insert at the outside edge. Smooth, even, and close stitching throughout. A soft lining with inverted seams. A flat insole. A noticeable curve in the last. No traces of glue. Shoes bend freely when flexed, then resume shape.

The Sole of Comfort. The line between dress and casual shoes has been crossed repeatedly by the Vibram sole—the lightweight rubbery outsole that takes ounces off shoes and adds spring and slip resistance to the step. Vibram was developed in 1938 by an Italian mountaineer, Vitale Bramani, who, having witnessed fellow climbers slip and fall to their deaths, set out to create surefootedness. Vibram has been a staple in mountaineering, trekking, and climbing shoes ever since. Its compounds are now adapted to specific environments, and maintain slip-resistance, for instance, even on ice and oil. In street shoes, air down clothes without taking the formality out of them altogether and flatter the leg by exposing much of the foot. Flats work with anything—skirts, pants, and leggings—and can be used as an eccentric accent. More classic tailored styles, such as the two-tone, can withstand extremes of color and pattern—even wildcat prints. **Shoe Care.** Leather breathes and needs a day or two after being worn to dry out. The same shoes should not be worn day after day. Alternate shoes if you want them to last. Polishing leather prevents it from cracking; shoe trees maintain shape. Reheel and resole when at all necessary.

well-dressed? Look down."

GEORGE FRAZIER

is added to the sole to reduce its weight. The latest variation on Vibram is Gumlite—a sole with the surefootedness of rubber but half the weight—developed for bucks and saddle shoes. **The Runner's Wing Tip** pushes the dress shoe ever further into lightweight, springy comfort with running shoe technology. As sneaker-bred generations fill the work force, manufacturers have attached cushioned soles and shock-absorbing heel cushions to otherwise businesslike oxfords. **Flats** offer fail-safe comfort for women: they dress

T-shirt

The most adaptable piece of clothing in Western civilization's wardrobe, the T-shirt is a sociological sponge and cultural bellwether of astounding accuracy. It has dismantled barricades between the classes and the sexes and moved in a matter of decades from lowly underwear for laborers to Oscar-ceremony garb. It has been on the front lines of war, protest, rock 'n' roll, sexual revolution, environmental crisis, and the advertising age. Printed, it is television for the body, a personalized broadcasting system that has issued "statements" from the ludicrous to the profound. Still, it remains uncorrupted, a reminder of simplicity, of sailors at sea, a utilitarian relief from the excesses of all it has encountered.

MOCK TURTLENECK   THE TANK   V-NECK   SLEEVELESS   CREW NECK

FABRIC

The personality of the T-shirt depends on fabric. A simple cotton tank top can become a luxury in silk. Cashmere, cashmere-linen blends, viscose, and rayon make the T-shirt a different proposition in each case. Cotton poorboy ribbing, popular in the Sixties, adds body.

T-BITS

The British navy was credited with originating the T-shirt when sailors were ordered to sew short sleeves on their sleeveless undershirts to screen hairy armpits from royal view.

The world's most copied T-shirt: The Gap Pocket T, first advertised on "individuals with style" in 1988. It is a retail sensation, defying all recessionary influences.

Clark Gable singlehandedly destroyed the undershirt market in 1934 when he stripped off his dress shirt in the film *It Happened One Night* to reveal a bare chest to Claudette Colbert. The gesture proved irresistible and American sales plummeted.

VOICE OF WISDOM

Giorgio Armani makes clothes that have a quiet authority. They never seem to raise their voice. They are softly constructed, in muted combinations of color and fabric. They move with the body. They are made to seem one with the wearer; never spanking new, but comfortable, at ease, broken-in.

The leader of Milanese ready-to-wear, Armani deconstructed the man-tailored suit, first for men, then for women. His slouchy androgyny was sought after, throughout the Eighties, by sophisticated executives of both sexes, and more recently by Hollywood stars, who flock to him. Called a classic designer, which he himself refutes, Armani has the knack of slightly veering his signature to the left or right each season in a way that remains true to himself, and the moment. As a result, his clothes are more about style than fashion and remain immune to recession, even at steep prices: over $1,000 for a cashmere blazer.

His signature is more affordable at Emporio Armani and, more recently, A/X (Armani Exchange)—warehouse-style stores that sell his jeans and utilitarian basics at a ceiling price of around $100 an item. Named to evoke the idea of a P/X or the military post exchanges of the Forties, A/X markets the civilian uniforms he himself wears: denim, twill pants with sweaters, white T-shirts.

He lives and works in an ascetic palazzo in Milan, a beach compound on the Mediterranean island of Pantelleria, a villa in Broni in northern Italy, and another in Forte di Marmi. He rarely wears jackets.

HIS UNIFORM

Khaki pants with
a navy sweater; jeans
and denim shirts,
white T-shirts.

CONTRIBUTIONS

Subtle style
Deconstructed jacket
Supple shape
Pantsuits for women

"Luxury is not overt. It comes in fabric,

PRINCIPLES OF DESIGN

"My personal philosophy is to ease clothes and maximize sensuality. I search for an image that's less aggressive, less avant-garde. Drastically imposing a fashion would mean having no respect for the consumer. As far as I am concerned, I do just the opposite: if I catch sight of a man or woman on the street dressed in a way that strikes me as uniquely elegant, I might interpret it for my collections. They label me the classic designer. But if you look at my clothes, they break every classic rule. On a classic jacket, the shoulders fit, the waist is marked—my jackets don't do any of that. "

SIMPLICITY

"Excess is always a mistake."

FIT

"A jacket should feel as comfortable as an old cardigan. It's something to feel relaxed in."

FABRIC

"The key to all design is an interest in fabric. There is always an element of movement in my clothes. Even if the fabric is heavy, it moves."

STYLE

"Style rises above fashion. It takes ideas and suggestions from fashion without swallowing them whole. There isn't a stylish man or woman who would radically alter their way of dressing for the sake of fashion."

QUALITY

"Quality distinguishes style from fashion."

color, proportion—things that last."

THE WHITE SHIRT

HAS ALWAYS BEEN A PRINCE AMONG SHIRTS: A SYMBOL OF THE GENTLEMAN BY VIRTUE OF PRISTINE COLOR.

Because it soiled so easily, it could only be worn by a man who, if he labored at all, did so as a "white-collar worker"—behind a desk. There is still little that rivals the combination of a white shirt and a dark suit for distinguished presentation. While office etiquette enforces less and less the hegemony of the white shirt over other colors, white provides the option of instant formality and can be kept on hand, pressed and waiting, in a desk drawer for evening or special events. For women, it is an element of simplification—dressy enough to stand on its own with a skirt or pants, and versatile with suits and sweaters. It presents a clean frame for the face and gives an edge of refinement to otherwise basic clothes.

SHIRT FABRICS. Quality dress shirts are of lightweight, finely woven cotton. The most luxurious are superfine cottons, such as long-staple Egyptian cotton and Sea Island cotton, which, because of longer fibers, create a sheer and satiny texture, at a price. Cotton poplin and broadcloth are suitably smooth weaves for city shirts. The less formal shirt takes a rougher weave such as oxford cotton, the fabric of the Brooks Brothers buttondown, which remains perfectly businesslike. Linen and cotton batiste, both sheer and lightweight, are comfortable in warm temperatures. Silk shirts are the most formal and are too refined for men to wear to the office, but not for women.

SIGNS OF QUALITY TAILORING

SINGLE-NEEDLE STITCHING

A more costly and time-consuming method of machine sewing which uses one needle to sew one side of a garment at a time, providing a consistent, careful stitch. The faster, less expensive method is to sew with double-needle stitching, working both sides of the garment at once, with a greater likelihood of puckering.

COLLAR

Evenly stitched around the edges

FIT

Sufficient blousiness in the sleeve. Where it joins the cuff, fabric should be gathered into pleats, not tapered.

BUTTONS

Cross-stitched and made of mother-of-pearl

A SPLIT-SHOULDER YOKE

A vertical seam down the yoke on the back of the shirt

GAUNTLET BUTTON

An anachronistic button on the sleeve opening, above the cuff

PLACKET

A count of fourteen stitches per inch on a shirt's placket—the strip of fabric on which the buttons are sewn—indicates quality. Fewer than eleven per inch signals lesser quality.

FRENCH CUFFS

To be worn with cuff links

LONG TAILS

Long enough to come together between the legs

Collars and Cuffs.

Like the silhouette of a suit, they set the tone of style. They signal the level of formality and the degree of quality in clothes, and are the determining cues that coordinate an outfit. As a rule, the stiffer the collar, the more formal the shirt. Both collars and cuffs are telltale signs of grooming and the level of care one takes with presentation. In aristocratic English circles, the frayed cuff and collar is a sign of eccentric disregard for dress. The customary attitude is to be critical of anything but the pristine. The habit of joining white collars and cuffs to a colored shirt, frequent among bankers, grew out of Victorian vigilance against dirt.

Collars are strategic frames for the face and should be matched to bone structure and the size of one's neck. (Cary Grant failed his first screen test because he was told that his 17-inch neck was too thick.) A narrow face looks best with a high collar of moderate spread; avoid long collars and thin ties. A broad face and full neck benefit, visually, from a low collar just covering the collarbone. Collars rise and fall with fashion; and the lengths of collars fluctuate with tie widths.

BARREL CUFFS

They are now the most common, because they are easy to manufacture. With one button, for business as well as leisure, they can accompany any collar, including the buttondown. With two buttons, they are more casual, and take a casual collar.

FRENCH CUFFS

Elegant and fairly formal, they are worn with business suits or black tie. They roll back from the wrist, are secured with links, and take a formal collar—a turn-down, cutaway, or pin.

QUALITY IN COLLARS

The workmanship that goes into a collar indicates the overall quality of the shirt. First, it should sit evenly on the neck. A well-made turndown collar will have a line of stitching around the edge as well as inner facing—a separate fabric insert, not a joined "fusible"—to give it shape. Puckering, in either stitching or fusing, is not a good sign. To determine collar size, measure the neck, just below the Adam's apple, with a tape measure and slip one finger inside the tape. Collars should fit snugly and should accommodate neckwear knots.

QUALITY IN CUFFS

Tapering a sleeve into a cuff is a tailoring shortcut. The better-made shirt retains the blousiness of the sleeve by joining it to the cuff with careful pleats and gathers. In England, custom shirtmakers sew small pleats in a complete circle around the cuff; in France, two or three pleats are tucked into the cuff on each side. The anachronistic detail of a gauntlet button, sewn into the sleeve placket along the slit that climbs the forearm, also signals quality. The button was at one time used for rolling back sleeves while washing.

THE ROUNDED (OR CLUB) COLLAR

Popularized by Eton schoolboys, worn high on the neck. Starched, it is dressy; soft, it's worn with sports jackets, and can be pinned or unpinned.

THE BUTTONDOWN

Adapted in 1900 by John Brooks of Brooks Brothers , the New York store, from the garb of English polo players. They wore formal cotton dress shirts with the collars buttoned down to keep them from flapping up during the match.

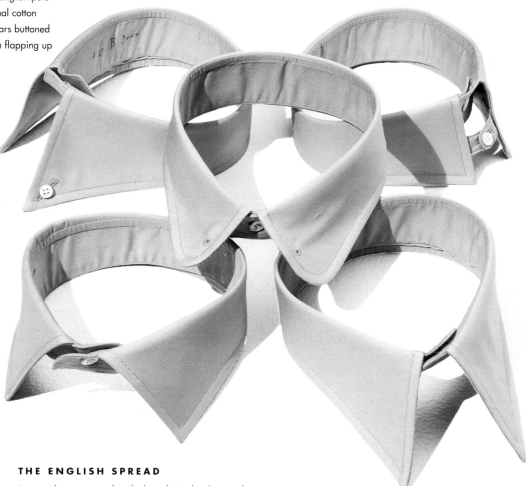

THE TAB COLLAR

First worn by the Duke of Windsor on a visit to the U.S.; now considered an American, Ivy League style, worn with blazers. The collar wings pull together to create a snug, neat line around the tie knot. Press fasteners have replaced brass studs.

THE ENGLISH SPREAD

Designed to accommodate the broad Windsor knot and a favorite of Prince Charles. Its formal cousin, the cutaway, is worn white, starched, and high on the neck.

THE STRAIGHT-POINT OR TURNDOWN COLLAR

The most innocuous, and therefore versatile. Lengths vary according to trends in lapel and tie size, but now hover between 2 5/8 and 2 7/8 inches.

Denim. Emblems of humility and hard work, denim and chambray shirts are worn in places they never used to be. Professional attire has relaxed to the extent that even these blue-collar work shirts, traditionally worn on the range or at sea, have acquired "white-collar" status in all but conservative offices. Despite the rule that a shirt be a shade lighter than the tie and suit it's paired with, indigo has become a business basic and has cleared the way for darker shirts of all colors. This turn in denim's fortunes could not have happened without stone-washing treatments that have made it gentler on the skin. Chambray, too, comes washed for softness. Denim shirts were previously the domain of cowboys, who buy them "rigid," or untreated and stiff. (Wrangler has sold them this way since 1949.) Chambray—a cooler, lighter-weight version of denim—has nautical roots, worn with white ducks by yachtsmen or as navy seamen's deck-swabbing gear. Both fabrics have an honesty and authenticity about them that appeal in the Nineties. The Amish, who aim to be "plain" in all things, wear chambray shirts.

WESTERN DETAIL
Long shirttails
Pearlized snaps
Three-button cuffs
Piped welt pockets
Fabric mixes

The yoke that dips to points in front and back on a Western shirt protects cowboys' shoulders from the sun with an extra layer of fabric.

Cowboy denim shirts are still sold untreated and stiff in Western specialty stores but are minor attractions compared to the more colorful, eccentric rodeo shirts real cowboys prefer. Unlike civilians, cowboys do not want a softened finish in a shirt. They prefer to stiffen their clothes with starch. "They look at a Western shirt that's been stonewashed and say, 'I have one I've had for five years that looks like that,'" says Joe Hertz, vice president and general manager of Wrangler shirts—the cowboys' brand. Authentic Western shirts worn by the approximately 10,000 working cowboys in the U.S. now take their cue from the inauthentic Western market—that styled by fashion designers such as Ralph Lauren. Dull plaids and stripes, and basic colors—acceptable to older cowboys—have given way to a new generation of wild color and bold prints. "The guys want to look great, with a little bit of flash and pizzazz," explains Dory Richardson of the Professional Rodeo Cowboys Association. In design, however, the real cowboy shirt, denim or otherwise, is made without a hem to prevent abrasion in the saddle.

TURTLENECKS.

SINCE NOËL COWARD SET THE PRECEDENT, MEN HAVE WORN turtlenecks as an escape from the obligation of shirt and tie. Nonconformist in style, they suggest Beats, loners, artists, and seafaring men. They are both austere and informal—a combination that makes them easy to wear. On women, too, a high-necked cashmere knit can be more elegant than sporty—a frame for the face that lengthens and conceals the neck. (The mock turtleneck abbreviates the height of the collar.) Cotton turtlenecks are more casual, and provide a layer of warmth and color under sweaters and flannel or denim shirts. The pullover, crew or V-necked, is another hardworking basic that can dress up or down, with jeans or a suit. Sleeker sweaters work as a color accent under sport coats. Pattern, in texture or color, raises the price of a sweater. Cashmere is a tempting investment, as it provides thermal control without bulk and feels luxurious.

POLO SHIRT

Designed for tennis in the early part of the century, the polo shirt has moved from sport to streetwear with charm, ease, and elegance. There is now a polo shirt for all climates and all occasions. Short-sleeved in cotton, long-sleeved in silk, it draws a natty collar line, free of stuffiness, beneath a jacket.

J e a n s . Since Levi Strauss invented blue jeans for the California Gold Rush miners over a century ago, a new species of clothing has been among us—one that is more serviceable, popular, and mythic than any garment in history. This assemblage of denim, copper rivets, and thread goes beyond the sum of its parts: it's the uniform of the individual—the ultimate in value.

More neutral than a fashion choice, jeans don't cover the body as much as they reveal it, take its form, fade and wear with idiosyncrasy. For all their rugged appeal and construction, they are illusory—an indigo canvas on which the zeitgeist has painted itself. They have dressed Americana: the farmer and the railway man and the hippie; the Marlboro Man and Elvis Presley; Gloria Vanderbilt and Andy Warhol. They have been a global emissary of democracy, a symbol of civil unrest, sexual revolution, and rock 'n' roll. They have suffered bell-bottoms, disco madness, "designer" labels, and the pummeling of stonewashing, only to emerge true to original form: the five-pocket Western jean—now preshrunk for comfort—has never been so popular. Dismantled dress

JEAN-IOLOGY

Levi's are defined in Webster's, enshrined in the Louvre, and displayed by the Smithsonian Institution as classic Americana.

HOT JEANS

Advertising brought sex out of the closet in 1980, when a fifteen-year-old Brooke Shields announced in TV spots for Calvin Klein jeans, shot by Richard Avedon, that nothing came between her and her Calvins, and if her Calvins could talk she'd be ruined. Responding to viewer criticism, stations in Los Angeles and New York banned some of the ads and restricted others to adult viewing hours.

codes are the jeans' boon, making them an accommodating "other" for anything one wants to wear, be it a tuxedo jacket, a T-shirt, or both. **Rivets and Levi's 501s.** The idea of securing jeans with rivets came from Jacob Davis, a Russian immigrant tailor in Nevada who persuaded Levi Strauss of the commercial potential of putting rivets on pants. Davis became Strauss's partner, and a patent for the rivets was granted to him in 1873. From it, in a few years, came a product called the "501 Double X blue denim waist overall" (501 was the lot number). The patent expired in 1908, when rival manufacturers started using rivets, but the 501 has remained virtually unchanged: still available in shrink-to-fit, heavyweight denim with a button fly. Rivets have been surpassed in fastening power by stitching, but jeans wearers continue to want them. In 1981, Levi's introduced 501 jeans cut for women, cut slightly broader through the hip.

"Denim is the one thing everyone owns."

DONNA KARAN

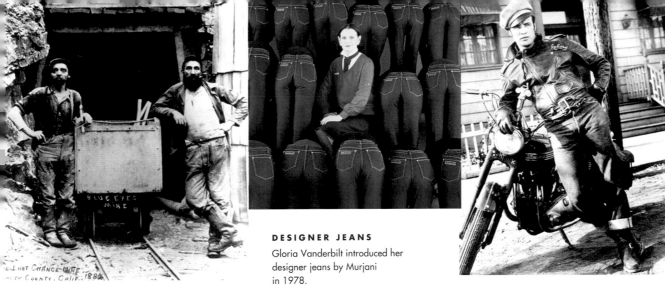

DESIGNER JEANS

Gloria Vanderbilt introduced her designer jeans by Murjani in 1978.

ROCK 'N' ROLL JEANS

Symbolic of sexual freedom, jeans' shock-value climaxed in 1971, in the Rolling Stones' *Sticky Fingers* album cover. The fly manually unzipped.

WORKING JEANS

When Levi Strauss, a Bavarian dry goods merchant, brought canvas for tents and wagon covers to the California Gold Rush in 1853, a prospector told him, "You should have brought pants." He returned with jeans of canvas, and miners took to wearing "those pants of Levi's."

REBEL JEANS

In the 1950s, Marlon Brando in *The Wild One* and James Dean in *Rebel Without a Cause* made jeans the hallmark of youth and rebellion.

WOMEN'S JEANS

According to the Lee company, the average woman tries on sixteen pairs of jeans before she finds one that fits well.

VOICE OF WISDOM

Zoran is the anomaly of American fashion: a designer who resists change in a business that thrives on it. He succeeds in wooing the most loyal, most elite clientele with anonymous elegance—an unchanging lexicon of minimalist clothes in luxurious fabrics: T-shirts, cashmere pullovers, and elastic-waisted pants. Amanda Burden, Lauren Hutton, Isabella Rossellini, Candice Bergen, and now, since he began selling in Milan, a roster of discreet Italian nobility have let him simplify their lives with autocratic authority. Since he began designing in 1976, his collections have barely budged from his original formula of five easy pieces, in a consistent palette of black, white, and beige, with the odd dash of red, bronze, or purple. His clothes are so undesigned, unadorned, and unconstructed as to disallow zippers or buttons. His one indulgence is fabric: silk, satin, and fine cashmere—often black—in the simplest pullovers, dresses, and wrap coats.

Yugoslavian-born Zoran Ladicorbic, forty-six, is fiercely bearded, contentious, and opinionated, but he swears allegiance to the middle ground—the Midwest, the all-American, the "normal." He vacations in spartan homes furnished with only mats on the floor in havens of manicured Americana—Naples, Florida, and Middleburg, Virginia. He regards sophistication in clothing as ambitious chicanery, and admires the great sartorial levelers who slayed frippery with style: Madame Mao (for having dressed all of China elegantly), Coco Chanel, and Giorgio Armani.

HIS UNIFORM

Black cashmere
sweaters
Black pants
Moccasins

CONTRIBUTIONS

A minimal wardrobe
Unconstructed
separates in luxury
fabrics

"There is no fashion wi

PRINCIPLES OF DESIGN

"Clothes today are about concept. My concept is that you can just build up your wardrobe and never throw things away. I decided to do good quality, so you're not buying anything that is frivolous and wearing it only once."

52

SIMPLICITY

"The longer you live, the simpler you become. You eliminate a lot in life, including friends."

WHAT CLOTHING SHOULD SAY ABOUT A PERSON

"Nothing."

THE UNIFORM

"A uniform is something for an intellectual person who doesn't have to worry about how they look. Madame Mao was the best designer. She designed the uniform for a billion people."

BASICS

"The T-shirt is the best American invention."

THE LUXURY OF UNDERSTATEMENT

"My clothes don't say anything, but you know that you're wearing cashmere. It looks like nothing, but feels like something. That becomes a luxury."

COMFORT

"Our brain needs comfort. When you irritate it, you cannot think."

thout personal style."

Gray Flannels. Of all

"odd" or unmatched trousers, gray flannels

have the most flexibility. Like the white flannels

of traditional English sport, they have an air of

the outdoors about them—rugged but

refined. They work with a variety of sports

jackets and colors from navy to muted

heathers. They are a sound investment. Like

cashmere, flannel has the feel of luxury without

the fussiness. Cuffs add drape and weight.

> "All a woman needs
> to be chic are a raincoat,
> two suits, a pair of
> trousers, and a
> cashmere sweater."
>
> HUBERT GIVENCHY

> "I wear pants
> almost exclusively
> so I can sit like a
> truck driver. I own
> one dress—a long
> evening gown."
>
> LAUREN
> BACALL

Khakis. Redolent with military mystique, khakis came into civilian use after World War II and take their name from the Hindi word for "dust-colored." Ideal summer trousers, they can, in heavier-weight cottons, move into spring and fall. Khakis are cut to have a baggy, carefree casualness, loose in the seat and upper thigh. Chinos are a close cousin, in a smoother all-cotton twill, also used in military uniforms. They come in a range of colors—black, gray, and white as well as khaki. Both have the kind of sporty classicism that can dress up with a navy sport coat, or down with knits, sweatshirts, and jean jackets. But even in the most casual combinations, khakis maintain a certain dignity.

A NAVY BLAZER IS ARGUABLY

THE MOST VERSATILE PIECE OF CLOTHING ONE CAN BUY. IT SIMPLIFIES

THROUGH FLEXIBILITY. IT CAN LOOK CRISP, TAILORED, AND ELEGANT WITH

a white shirt (and, for men, a tie) or played down with jeans and a T-shirt. It outfits a wardrobe for work or play,

and almost anything in between. Adapted from naval uniforms, the classic **double-breasted** blazer is

B L A

the only sports jacket that has metal buttons and, with them, a sense of occasion. Associated with mahogany-

decked yachts and boardrooms, it is a stylized version of the shorter "reefer" jacket worn in severe weather by

the British Royal Navy. (Navy has been the color of naval uniform around the globe since the eighteenth

century.) The **single-breasted** blazer, with patch pockets, is more casual, collegiate, and not always blue.

American campuses adopted it in the Twenties from the competitive attire of English university boating and

cricket clubs, where solid or striped jackets were ablaze with color. The patch breast pocket takes a college or club

crest. Quality in a blazer is determined by pristine cut, traditional fabric—such as flannel—and good buttons.

Tall tales of the blazer's birth. The captain of a British frigate, the H.M.S. *Blazer*, was so alarmed by the motley appearance of his crew on the eve of Queen Victoria's coronation that he ordered them into spiffy navy jackets with brass buttons, designed after the sailor's short "reefer." The Queen so approved that she made them part of the navy's official uniform. No doubt the blazer's double-breasted design springs from naval costume. But the name is more definitively rooted in the colorful single-breasted jackets worn by cricketers and rowers at Cambridge and Oxford in the late nineteenth century, which is said to have inspired the comment, "Bit of a blazer, what?" At regattas such as Henley, the blazer is worn with a boater and flannel trousers. **The 1915 Brooks Brothers catalogue** lists a "single-breasted flannel Blazer for tennis, cricketing, etc." But the blazer did not fully take root in American soil until 1920, when it showed up at Ivy League colleges such as Harvard, Yale, and Princeton, and in Newport on college men on vacation. **Linked to the boardroom,** the resort, and the Establishment, the blazer is good at signaling old school ties through crested buttons and breast pocket patches denoting clubs or associations.

Z E R

"A classic has to be made of excellent fabric, in a color that can outlast fashion and, most important, it's cut to emphasize tradition."

GIORGIO ARMANI

ANATOMY OF THE CLASSIC BLAZER
double-breasted with six metal buttons, only two of which, on the lower right, actually function. The rest are for show. It has side vents, two flap pockets, a breast pocket, and peaked lapels cut horizontally, with a buttonhole in each.

BLAZER FABRICS
doeskin flannel, wool serge, cashmere, worsted, linen, or blended fabrics.

BLAZER BUTTONS
brass, silver, or gold. If they are smooth they should be flat. Those that don't actually button are fastened to the inside of a jacket by cutting a hole in the fabric and securing them from the inside. Expensive buttons are removed for dry cleaning.

"One shouldn't spend all one's time dressing. All one needs are two or three suits, as long as they, and everything to go with them, are perfect."

COCO CHANEL

In conservative circles, brown is less than appropriate for business suits.

Navy, the traditional color of European and English banking suits, is impeccable. Gray is the bulwark color of corporate America.

A double-breasted jacket must stay buttoned while the wearer is standing, and does not take a "waistcoat," the British term for vest.

Climate control is built into the finest wools now available: they breathe in warm weather, insulate in cool weather, and resist wrinkling throughout. Keep in mind that most lightweight summer fabrics highlight flaws in tailoring.

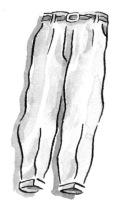

SUITS.

SINCE CHARLES II ORDERED THE THREE-piece suit to be the uniform of the day in 1666, the suit has been the backbone of basics. It is now fundamental to women's wardrobes as well as to men's. Its strictly corporate connotations have loosened in recent years with a comfort revolution that has added sensuality to fabric and cut. Suits are no longer stiff or one-dimensional. They move into all areas of life and cover more ground than any other sartorial investment. The fit and cut of the jacket are both important. The modern ideal follows the contour of the body and moves with the fluidity of a sweater. Superfine, high-performance wools have made men's suits much less confining, and wrinkle-free. In concept as well as fabric, suits are no longer a constraint. They open up possibilities.

"I come from a tailoring family and I grew up with things made specifically for me from age five. I write like a tailor which is with care to detail. Good tailoring is very subtle tailoring. You don't see the workmanship—you feel it more than you see it. When you're in a well-constructed page of writing you feel the fit, the careful balance of the rhythm of the sentence. Understatement is a quality of fine writing."

GAY TALESE

Dior made it a vehicle of the New Look, above, in the '40s.

The actress Jean Eagles was known for coming to rehearsal every day in the same black
jersey dress. Ruth Gordon visited her at home one evening, where Eagles greeted her in the same black
dress. "Don't you have any other dresses?" Gordon asked. Eagles said, "Come and see my closet."
In it were hanging about twenty versions of the same black dress.

As told by **GLORIA VANDERBILT**

THE BLACK DRESS.

SINCE COCO CHANEL FIRST CREATED IT IN THE TWENTIES, THE LITTLE BLACK DRESS HAS SPRUNG UP IN EVERY decade. The original anti-fashion item of the twentieth century, it mimicked the uniforms of shop girls and waitresses—anonymous and unadorned. It gave evening clothes the attitude of tennis dresses, was made to be worn with the Twenties "debutante slouch," and came in a color previously reserved for mourning. Chanel designed it in black crepe marocain or crepe de chine, matched with a neat, small hat for the cocktail hour—a new American social pastime. It possessed what Balzac called "the luxury of simplicity." *Vogue* magazine labeled it Chanel's "Ford," a utilitarian vehicle of the mechanized age. In recent memory, the little dress has turned voluptuous in body-sculpting stretch fabrics. Black is the bulwark of its success: the only truly basic color, at once formal and informal, it puts the focus on the face, slims the body, and conceals imperfect tailoring.

Formalwear. Perhaps the most flattering clothing known to man, the proper tuxedo is grace incarnate in women's eyes, as smooth as a dance with Fred Astaire. Strictly speaking, formal occasions such as state dinners and some weddings require white tie or full dress: tails for evening or morning coats for day. Black tie is actually semi-formal, but it's the only formal attire most people are likely to wear. Tuxedos, or dinner jackets

What the English call a dinner jacket and the French "*un smoking*" is a "tuxedo" in America, due to the events of a single evening. In the late nineteenth century, Griswold Lorillard, scion of the American tobacco family, attended a country club ball in

The Duke of Windsor determined midnight blue to be the most flattering color for a dinner jacket. To his keen eye, black took on a greenish cast in artificial light, while midnight blue appeared "blacker than black." He also introduced comfort into black tie with soft pleated shirt fronts and turned-down collars in place of stiff boiled shirts, and in the Thirties he did away with the vest by setting a trend for double-breasted dinner jackets.

T U X E D O

as they are called in England, are more often rented than purchased. However, if you have occasion to wear black tie more than three times a year, it pays to buy one. Like all suits, it can be taken apart. If your tuxedo is your own, you will have more occasion to put a personal stamp on it—to wear the jacket with jeans, à la Andy Warhol, or the trousers with a black cardigan sweater, for a more relaxed look. The classic style is always a better investment. Overly wide or narrow lapels and fabrics other than wool are best avoided, as they date easily.

Tuxedo Park, the exclusive community outside of New York City. He wore a velvet smoking jacket like one his tailor had made for the Prince of Wales, later Edward VII. A much more youthful, insouciant style of evening attire than customary, "what they were wearing in Tuxedo," as the press described it, caused a sensation amid top hats and tails, and soon retired the tail-coat to full dress.

Peaked versus Notched Lapels. The peak-lapelled, single-breasted dinner jacket, derived from the original tailcoat, is the most correct form of black tie. The notched lapel, like that of a business suit, has infiltrated formal attire only because it costs less and is more convenient to manufacture. As a result, notched lapels are now mistaken for classic form, and are more affordable and available than the peaked. Shawl collars are authentically classic, if old guard, and double-breasted closure is an acceptable alternative to the single-breasted jacket.

BLACK TIE BASICS

WAISTCOAT

Antecedent of the cummerbund, worn with scooped lapels in decorative silks

TROUSERS

Without belt loops, worn with suspenders or "braces." They are never cuffed; cuffs were devised as rural mud-catchers. The satin seam up the leg is a relic of the braid on officers' uniforms.

PUMPS

Perhaps derived from the word "pomp," in patent leather, with grosgrain bows, or in monogrammed velvet. Plain-toe oxfords, in calfskin or patent leather, are an alternative. Both take calf-length black socks in silk or lightweight wool.

SCARF

In white silk or a silk pocket square

JACKET

Without vents, in wool, with buttons covered in fabric to match the satin lapels or made of matte black bone. Styles are single- or double-breasted.

DRESS SHIRT

Colored white, sometimes ivory. With a wing collar, the shirt takes a stiff piqué bosom and single cuffs. With a turndown collar, it has a pleated front and double French cuffs.

CUMMERBUND

Instead of a waistcoat, in black or colored silk, brocade or moiré, worn always with pleats facing up, originally to hold theater tickets

TIE

Of modest width, in black silk or satin or a color that coordinates with the cummerbund

JEWELRY

studs and cuff links, in mother of pearl, pearl, black onyx, silver, or white gold

WOMEN AND THE TUX. Marlene Dietrich, Judy Garland, Princess Diana, and Catherine Deneuve have all worn black tie to androgynous advantage. Details women have borrowed from this masculine archetype include: wing-collared, pleated-front shirts, soft bow ties, cummerbund belts, patent-leather flats with bows, and monogrammed velvet or suede slippers. Yves Saint Laurent has been the greatest proponent of black tie, or "*le smoking*," for women. His feminine dinner jackets are worn with collarbones bared, over skirts or trousers.

TRENCH COAT.

ESPIONAGE. MYSTERY. LONERS IN THE MIST. DRAMA AND INTRIGUE have pursued the trench coat since it was created for British army officers in World War I. The idea of Englishman Thomas Burberry, one of the world's first weatherproof-fabric technicians, it's made for the rigors of the trenches, with wool-lined, water-resistant cotton gabardine—Burberry's invention—and functional detail. Militaristic intent has not interfered with the total integration of the trench coat into civilian life and even high fashion—reissued in luxury fabrics from black satin to gold lamé, for day or evening, in full or three-quarter length. In the cinema, it has evoked charisma since Humphrey Bogart wore it on the airstrip in *Casablanca*. The undercover cool of the anti-hero, the unsung Resistance fighter, or the enlisted officer in the battle of life has clung to it ever since. Armies of detectives, spies, and traveling salesmen have adopted it, from the tragic (Willy Loman) to the comic (Columbo and Inspector Clouseau). It has the kind of anonymity that conceals, one suspects, the utterly desirable.

The Burberry Brainstorm.

Thomas Burberry, who opened his sportswear business in England in 1856, conceived of the trench coat as a healthful—breathable—alternative to the rubber-lined mackintosh. He even consulted a doctor who confirmed that it would be better to be drenched in rain than sweaty condensation. He took inspiration from the linen frock smocks of English shepherds, the close weaves of which kept out moisture. He improved on them with tight weaves of cotton and wool which he named "gabardine," after Shakespeare's description of Caliban's coat in *The Tempest*. Gabardine was shelter from the storm, precisely because it allowed air to pass through it. With it, he made clothes for nineteenth-century adventure: balloon ascents, expeditions to the poles and "out" to India and the British colonies. Captain Roald Amundsen, leader of the first successful expedition to the South Pole, left a tent in Burberry's gabardine on his campsite to notify his rivals that he had gotten there first. Of Burberry's gabardine, which he wore as expedition overalls, he said, "It is extraordinarily light and strong and keeps the wind completely out." Burberry's classic model has sold more than a million since 1917.

CRUMPLED CHARISMA

Bogie in *Casablanca*

UNISEX APPEAL

As pioneered by Marlene
Dietrich in *Foreign Affair*

**TO THE
TRENCHES**

The trench coat as
WWI uniform

SLEUTH APPAREL

Peter Sellers as
Inspector Clouseau in
The Pink Panther

WOOL-LINED COLLAR

Turns up to protect the neck

BUTTONED-DOWN EPAULET

Served to secure a rifle over the shoulder

LINING

Detachable, made of
wool

**SEPARATE
BACK YOKE**

For rain protection

STORM FLAP

Buttons over the chest

CLOTH BELT

Usually worn tied, not buckled,
it has metal rings from which to
hang grenades and canteens

BUCKLED CUFF

Battens out the wind

STYLE

ELEMENTS

THE ELEMENTS OF STYLE ARE THE ABSOLUTES THAT

OF

COHERE UNDER THE INFLUENCE OF VISION AND ATTITUDE.

STYLE

FIT: The shaping that marries clothes to the body, for better or worse. Fit defines proportion and silhouette; it determines appropriateness. It can flatter or flabbergast and it should follow function. Whether classically tailored or deconstructed, oversize or snug, fit determines whether clothes work. COMFORT: Without it, clothes stay in the closet. Standards of comfort improve each decade under the influence of technology, human nature, and changed dress codes. Comfort now drives fashion and the design of all kinds of clothes from business suits to mountaineering gear. COLOR: Style's expressive plaything as well as its hardworking tool. Color coordinates clothing, and from its base a wardrobe is built. FABRIC: The starting point from which stylistic revolution grows. It defines the limitations of design and whether clothes can live up to their intentions. It determines quality and durability as well as ease of wear. Fabric technology has pushed comfort into the twenty-first century. APPROPRIATENESS: The degree to which form follows function or deliberately deviates from it. Purpose-packed garments, especially in high-tech activewear, have proliferated, but so has license to exercise individuality through idiosyncratic combination. PRACTICALITY: How far one is willing to go for appearance before comfort, common sense, and budget intervene. The usefulness of a garment, determined by asking where and when one would wear it, and how it would work with the clothes you own. VALUE: Insurance that clothing will last and serve you well, given the purchasing power of your budget. Versatility is a component.

VOICE OF WISDOM

Geoffrey Beene is the "couturier" of Seventh Avenue. Ease—modern and all-American—is the achievement of his design career, and for that he has won more Coty Awards than any other American designer. His clothes are driven by comfort, innovative cut, and a blurring of distinctions between day and evening wear, between the luxurious and the comfortable. Jackie Kennedy Onassis, Gloria Steinem, and Faye Dunaway all travel with his evening gowns rolled in their suitcases; the dresses emerge unruffled.

Since he founded his own business in 1963, he has aimed to decompartmentalize fashion: to mix the refined fabric—silk or lace—with the ordinary workaday wool jersey; to make coats reversible from day into night; to banish rules about time and place in clothing. In the Seventies, he brought sportswear out at night with sweatshirt and sequined jersey dresses. Trained as a doctor, he makes clothes follow the body with fluid form.

A Southern gentleman who cultivates orchids in his spare time, Beene seduces with witty detail and flashes of color in accessories, the lining of a coat, or the underside of a garment only the wearer herself will see. He loves pattern, stripes, and the vivid, graphic power of black and white. "I'm crazy about dots," he drawls. He is a radical pragmatist, a realist, and everything he touches, no matter how pretty or gay, succumbs to utter utility, service, and comfort.

HIS UNIFORM

"I wear a collarless shirt, pleated pants, and comfortable shoes. I hate jackets."

CONTRIBUTIONS

American elegance

Jersey evening dresses that roll up into a suitcase

The toga dress

Pajama pants

"Luxury need not have a pric

PRINCIPLES OF DESIGN

"I like to make clothes that have something very friendly, something amusing or jarring that is very personal to a woman. Other people may never see it— like a colorful lining of a coat. There's a lot of liquid geometry in my clothes."

HOW TO INVENT STYLE

" I would advise a woman to buy anything simple and let her elaboration begin. You can embellish with accessories. It's sometimes the simplest thing. A big massive bracelet, the kind that comes from Africa, makes a statement, as opposed to two hundred tiny ones."

HOW TO BUILD A WARDROBE

"Start with a color. Black frames anything that's around it. It defines line, it defines silhouette. It shows architectural form. You can add to it, take from it. The amount of black doesn't matter, it's the amount of other color that matters."

COMFORT

"The sweatshirt equates comfort, which is what modern clothes should be."

e—comfort itself is a luxury."

fabric

IT ALL BEGINS HERE. FABRIC PROVIDES THE ORIGINAL LINK BETWEEN

SKIN AND CLOTHING, AND AS SUCH, IS THE KEY TO COMFORT. SUBTLETY

IS FABRIC'S TRIUMPH, PULLED OFF IN TONE-ON-TONE WEAVES,

surface pattern, textural contrasts, and gradients of touch. One may prefer dry linen to liquid silk, ornate

jacquard to rugged denim. But however ornamental, fabric's form is grounded in function. It is highly

engineered and comfort-driven, and its technology is the root of all stylistic revolution. Du Pont's sortie

into nylon in 1937 produced the "nylon" stocking, later tights, which still later were blended with Lycra

for a snug, resilient fit. Qiana nylon emerged twenty years ago to fuel the development of ski and

"For the first forty years of my life I wore pajamas under my trousers.
No one knows why including me."

BUCK HENRY

outdoor clothes, now superseded by a mindboggling array of high-tech fibers— lightweight weatherproof insulators— vying to be recognized by their patented trade- marks. New knits and woven fabrics have made softened tailoring and jackets that fit like sweaters a given for men and women. With microfibers, synthetics have finally lost their second-class standing against natural fibers, however much diehard naturalists may resist. Wrinkle-free and breathable microfiber is twice as fine as the finest silk. It is luxurious to the touch, and has been hailed as the biggest development in fabric since the Chinese discovered the silkworm.

SUPER YARNS

The difference between Super 100's wool and rough, heavy tweed is length of fiber: a pound of Super 100's can be spun into a thread 30 miles long. However long and delicate, the fiber is strong and the fabric woven from it extremely lightweight.

Taken from merino sheep in Australia (formerly bred in Tasmania), super-fine wool is graded according to an English system of measure, for strength, tenacity, and color.

Twill, the most durable and tightly woven of men's fabrics, combines the ultimate in luxury and utility when woven in a superfine wool. "Tasmanian," the trademarked name of Loro Piana's super-fine twill, is an example.

WONDER WOOL: SUPER 100'S

In the beginning, it was called "priest cloth"—fine, lightweight, all-season wool woven for members of the Vatican by the Italian textile firm Loro Piana. Now Super 100's wool and the fabric woven from it have been made into suits as soft as silk pajamas. They weigh half as much as the serge sack suits of old. They travel without creasing or losing shape, and are comfortable in summer and winter. While the Italians were the first to spin very fine wool into fiber, Super 100's (and lesser grades numbered Super 60's, 70's, and 80's) has gained currency in the U.S. in the last five years. Regardless of grade, wool is inherently wrinkle- resistant due to fiber structure; it breathes naturally, absorbs moisture in the heat, and insulates against the cold. Fabrics of fine wool have exceptional "memory"—they bounce back when stretched, as well as drape and retain body.

POLYESTER MEETS THE MICROFIBER

When polyester, the much maligned invention of the early Fifties, emerged in the form of the infamous lounge suit, a television ad showed a man bathing, sleeping, and eating in his suit day after day, without making a wrinkle in his garment. That gruesome reputation for drip-dry durability could not be further from the reality of polyester microfiber as it exists today: soft, supple, lightweight but strong, it is both breathable and water-repellent. Like natural fibers, it "wicks" or draws moisture away from the body. Du Pont first developed the technology to create microfibers in the Sixties: polyester polymer is forced through the microscopically small holes of a spinneret to produce a single filament per hole; these filaments make up a polyester microfiber yarn that can be blended with cotton, silk, or rayon. In the Eighties, European designers such as Claude Montana and Yves Saint Laurent brought microfiber into fashion. In the U.S., microfiber (in polyester, nylon, and acrylic) has made clothes at once practical and luxurious. In texture, microfiber can feel like chamois, washed silk, satin, taffeta, or velvet and produces an exceedingly vivid printed image. For all of this, one does pay a price. It is twice as expensive as conventional polyester.

TAILORING

BEGAN WITH THE RENAISSANCE AND

its pursuit of humanism, or concern for life this side of the hereafter. Clothes went from concealing the body in the Middle Ages to celebrating it. Cutting fabric and shaping it to the human form became a highly skilled craft; tailoring flourished alongside the arts and sciences, and the practice of medicine, to which it remains linked in curious ways. Both Giorgio Armani and Geoffrey Beene, two of the most distinguished fashion designers working today, were originally students of the body, trained as doctors. The Savile Row area of London—the locus of tailoring tradition— housed the offices of physicians and surgeons before tailors crowded them out early in the nineteenth century.

TAILOR TALK Drop: the chest measurement minus the waist measurement. The longer the drop, the trimmer one has to be to wear it well. **Break:** the horizontal ripple in the trouser leg where it touches the top of the instep, as well as the crease across the top (or vamp) of a shoe. **Drape:** how the fabric hangs from the shoulder or waist. **Inseam:** the length of the inside of the leg, cuff to crotch. **Rise:** the distance between the crotch and the waistband.

CUSTOM FIT

A Savile Row suit requires an average of three fittings, with a minimum of twenty measurements taken for the jacket alone. Suits are fitted with all accessories—wallets, keys—in place. Trousers require at least five more measurements, and patterns are kept for future reference. Buttonholes take four hours to complete.

Fred Astaire had good tailoring. The suit held on to his leaps across the room. When good tailors make suits, they don't just fit you standing, they fit you walking, stretching, soaring.

GAY TALESE

TAILORING WISDOM from Martin Greenfield, eminent American tailor and suit manufacturer. **On Style:** "People no longer like the old way of having a tailored suit made. We used to finish it, press it, and it would practically stand up by itself. Everything was molded to the body so it looked like a suit of armor. Today people want the opposite: comfort and light weight." **How to Recognize Quality:** "If a suit is well made, I can separate the three plies of fabric when I touch it: the outside shell, the inner facing now lightweight canvas, and underneath I'd like to feel a Bemberg lining that feels like silk. If I looked around the inside of the armhole, I'd see handstitching. The underside and the outside of the collar would be sewn by hand along with the buttonholes. There's no substitute for the flexibility handstitching gives you. When you put your hand in the pockets of the jacket and trousers, you should feel fine cotton. In every good suit, pockets should last forever. Inside, the waistband of the trousers should be the same fabric as the pocket lining and it should have genuine horn buttons."

SIGNS OF QUALITY TAILORING IN A JACKET

COLLAR

Smooth and flat against the neck

HANDSTITCHING

At the collar and sleeve, stresspoints strategic to the fit. Stitches will be visible beneath the collar at the back of the neck, and around the inside armhole. The more stitches per inch, the better quality the tailoring.

A CLOTHING CANVAS

Inserted between the lining and the fabric to give the jacket an even, flat contour. The lesser-quality suit, and most that are ready-made, achieves contouring through fusing, or heat-welding the fabric at the risk of puckering. If the lapel of a jacket feels of a single piece when you rub it between thumb and forefinger, a "fusible" has probably been used.

SHOULDER LINE

Smooth from end to end

FABRIC

Soft, and pliant to the touch

LAPEL

Lies perfectly flat without buckling

SLEEVE

Set without puckering to hang slightly forward, tapering gently from the shoulder to the hem; neither too tight nor too full

POCKETS

Lined in cotton

INSIDE POCKET

Roomy enough to hold accessories

LINING

In silky Bemberg rayon, proferably full length

PATTERN

It should always line up without interruption across pockets and seams.

SEAMS

In an unconstructed jacket without a lining, look for seams that are taped, without ragged edges. (Double-faced fabrics obviate the need for a lining in this type of tailoring.)

BUTTONHOLES

Hand-sewn and smooth on the outside, rough on the inside

BUTTONS

In genuine horn

SIGNS OF QUALITY TROUSERS: a "crotchpiece" lining that covers the meeting of seams to absorb stress and reduce chafing; a fully constructed waistband that doesn't curl over, made with a piece of clothing canvas inserted between the shell fabric of the waistband and its lining (this won't be visible, but it should feel both firm and pliable); cotton-lined waistband and pockets.

QUALITY EQUALS VALUE

"Good taste shouldn't have to cost anything extra."

MICKY DREXLER,
president of The Gap, Inc.

Quality does not depend on the amount of money spent, but on the value received. That value is ultimately a subjective assessment, dependent in part on one's budget, degree of need, and aesthetic satisfaction. But there are some likely vehicles of value. Classics earn their name on the back of utility and elegance, delivered consistently over time. Less is automatically more when versatility is involved: an expensive suit that can be worn in many ways, throughout the year, is less costly in the end than a closet full of inflexible "bargains." Quality's ultimate value is the serenity that comes with style.

"I have worked in the fashion industry for a long time," says the former Chanel model who has launched her own fashion business. "Just like everyone else, I work, I go out, and every morning, I must find something to wear—something that suits me, in which I feel comfortable all day long. In the past, I have had closets so full they could burst. Now I prefer to have only a few things, but good ones."

INÈS DE LA FRESSANGE

The de la Fressange guiding principles: **Principle No. 1** "Start with garments that already exist: a real blazer, a twin set. The type of straight-forward no-nonsense item that should be a staple of any wardrobe." **Principle No. 2** "Demand the highest standard of quality for these clothes, not only for cut, but detail work, and finishing." **Principle No. 3** "I look for a basic range of colors and the very best in fabrics." **Principle No. 4** "I disregard the idea of trends changing automatically from one season to the next. My wardrobe evolves gradually, with subtle updates and in accordance with my lifestyle."

OPTIONS

"It has long been an axiom of mine that the little things are infinitely the most important."

SHERLOCK HOLMES

Sustaining style on a daily basis is easier with options—the free-floating elements that diversify a wardrobe of basics, that apply a personal stamp, a jolt of the unexpected, and, in the long run, economy through versatility. A scarf, a vest, or a sweater reinvent themselves, depending on the way they are worn. Color and pattern come into play as accents that only you would choose. Small things are often noticed first. Whether an expensive piece of jewelry or a trinket, accessories leave a determining mark and can mood-alter clothes into a new dimension. A sense of proportion and of play help: heaps of pearls or a single strand? A big bag or a little one? Options are a wardrobe's bookends: they frame and position clothes and signal attitude.

Striped Shirts. While fads for pattern in shirts come and go, stripes remain a classic, though they entered the gentleman's wardrobe in 1870 with some outcry. Known as "regatta shirts," they were deemed unsuitable for business wear, as they were suspected of being worn in order to disguise dirt. The pinstripe, lined up like the columns of an accountant's ledger, is now synonymous with finance—be it that of the banker or the gangster. The narrower the stripe, the more conservative the shirt. Stripes tend to widen with physical activity: the broadest stripe adorns the rugby shirt.

PATTERN has proliferated in men's shirts, relaxing suits and stirring up color. However, there are some rules. Patterns are most effectively combined when they are of different scales. A broad-striped tie works best with a fine-striped shirt; a glen plaid sports jacket can take a boldly striped shirt. The point is to avoid competing patterns: let one dominate.

In plaids, generally, the smaller the pattern, the less strenuous the activity for which it is worn. Small checks are worn easily to the office as well as to fish or golf. Larger checks are linked with lumberjacks, and faded madras with gentlemanly sports. The more ethnic or exotic the pattern, the less rigid the dress code.

CHALK STRIPE

PINSTRIPE

PENCIL STRIPE

HAIRLINE STRIPE

B e l t s make clothes more casual, Coco Chanel maintained. She had a point. On men, belts encode formality, much like shoes, through color and material: black leather is the most formal, brown less so, and cloth or webbing is casual. Business wear cannot tolerate much exuberance in this item; discretion serves, especially in the buckle. The more casual the attire, the more expressive the belt can be.

For both sexes, the level of quality is conspicuous in this accessory, and it's wise to buy a more expensive belt as an investment that can work with much of your clothing. The most versatile are the least boisterous—not bland but subtly interesting. Ethnicity can lend a certain validity to excesses of form. For instance, the classic Western belt can carry off the extravagance of an Indian silver buckle.

THE TIE

HAS BEEN HAUNTED BY PREDICTIONS OF IMMI-nent doom for decades and still it dangles on. And there are reasons. However inessential, the tie provides a rare service of ornamentation in a man's wardrobe, much like that performed by jewelry for women. By width alone, it can update a suit without great expense, and allows for variety, color, and texture. Perversely for such a supercilious item, the tie carries with it a culture-load of associations which, in the hierarchical business world, will not drop away easily. Especially in Britain, the old school tie, or ties that carry the colors, stripes, and crests of a particular scholastic, sporting, social, or military institution, are flashed as flags of introduction and affiliation—signs of belonging. The classic rep tie (a corded silk with diagonal stripes) is less likely to carry such encoded significance in the U.S., but it makes a conservative statement nonetheless, depending on its color.

In texture and fabric, the tie should set the tone of an ensemble. A nubby wool sport coat takes an even nubbier wool or knit tie; a smooth suit takes an even smoother silk tie.

THE UNIVERSAL TIE

If you want to own only one tie, the black silk knit tie is everyman's ally. It simplifies life by going anywhere, with ease and elegance. It works in any context, with any kind of shirt, patterned or solid, in denim or Egyptian cotton, with a blazer or a leather jacket. It travels without wrinkling. Stains are less visible on its textured surface, and it can be worn daily without risk of error in color or combination.

"I don't know what purpose a tie serves—and I sell ties, and lots of them."

GEOFFREY BEENE

TIE-ING it all together. The tie takes its cue from the shirt, and that combination sets the tone for other accessories—socks, shoes, and belts. Ties also coordinate with shirt collars. Tab and pin-collared shirts take smaller knots; the spread collar accommodates larger neckties and full or half Windsor knots.

QUALITY. Except for those in knit, good ties will be interlined with muslin to provide enough bulk for knotting. The muslin can be felt under the lining. **Examine the bar tack,** a short horizontal stitch on the back of the broad end of the tie that keeps it from gaping. It should be neat, and should not show signs of pulling at the fabric around it. **The well-tied tie** will have a slight dimple in the middle of it beneath the knot.

KNOTS. The four-in-hand is the simplest and produces a discreet, low-lying knot, standard in the U.S. **The Windsor** is a more protrusive, decorative knot popularized by the Duke of Windsor, who liked his ties to jut forward from a spread collar. A full or half Windsor knot requires many more twists and turns than the four-in-hand.

PATTERNS. The Club tie has a dark ground with heraldic patterns or crests. **The Regimental stripe** or "Rep" tie of rep silk has diagonal stripes in the colors and widths of British military regiments. **The Foulard** is of lightweight silk twill with small geometric prints. **The Grenadine** is of loosely woven silk knit with an irregular surface. **The Challis** is of a wool worsted, patterned or solid.

Suspenders. "Braces," as the British call them, acquired a bad rap in the Eighties as symbols of stock market madness, and Gekko-esque greed (as in the movie *Wall Street*). Deemed showy by some, they serve the real function of making trousers hang a bit more smoothly than they would if belted, and with more comfort. The most secure suspenders button rather than clip on to waistbands. They also add color, to be coordinated with tie pattern.

The arguments for wearing suspenders are persuasive: they are unconstricting and allow pants to hang loosely around the body.

Quality suspenders are made in rayon with leather fittings. Straps that are 1 ¼ to 1 ½ inches wide are most comfortable. Trousers need to have four buttons in front and two in back sewn into the waistband to take suspenders.

The vest. Part accessory, part suit, the vest is at once decorative and tailored. It can pull together the most casually assembled outfit, and give even jeans and T-shirts the coherence of style. The third wheel of the three-piece suit until war restrictions banned its production in the Forties, the vest has reemerged as a versatile, unisex item in its own right. In light fabrics, it's a summer alternative to a jacket; women can wear it as a bodice with nothing beneath. With jeans, it has Western authenticity—cowboys wore vests to tote their tobacco in the saddle. It can dress up and down, often simultaneously. However flamboyant, in silk brocades or leopard spots, it retains, through tailoring, classic appeal. Beau Brummell, the nineteenth-century dandy, made his sartorial splash in part by spurning the decorated vests of his day for those in white.

UNISEX CHARM

In *Annie Hall* in the Seventies

A SPLASH OF COLOR

The yellow vest sings in the rain on Gene Kelly.

THE BOTTOM BUTTON

According to English tailoring tradition, this button must always be worn undone. The style was set, probably inadvertently, by King Edward VII, and lingers on to the extent that English tailors cut vests so that the bottom button does not fasten.

FIT

Vests should fit cleanly over the body and cover the waistband of trousers.

DUELING PATTERNS

The Sixties vest on Sonny, with Cher

TALL IN THE SADDLE

The cowboy vest on John Wayne

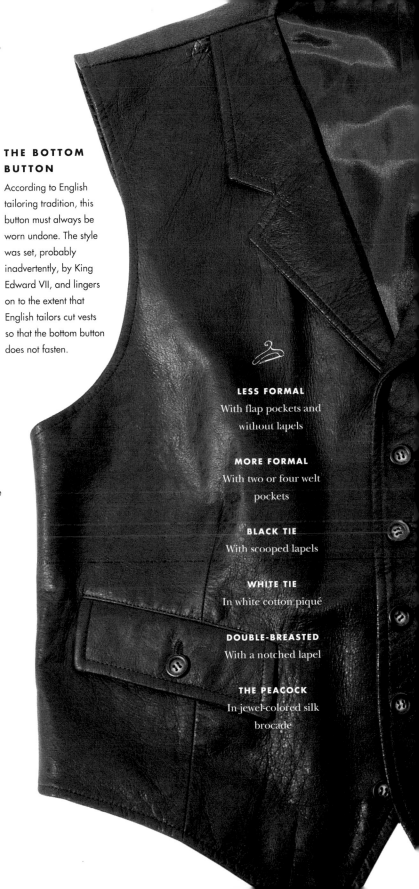

LESS FORMAL

With flap pockets and without lapels

MORE FORMAL

With two or four welt pockets

BLACK TIE

With scooped lapels

WHITE TIE

In white cotton piqué

DOUBLE-BREASTED

With a notched lapel

THE PEACOCK

In jewel-colored silk brocade

VOICE OF WISDOM

Coco Chanel. The great French couturière, Gabrielle "Coco" Chanel, took fussiness and pretension out of high fashion and exchanged it for style. She redefined luxury as simplicity, and elegance as practicality, ease, and comfort. She charted modernity in clothes, and dressed a dynamic, active woman (the flapper) who drove cars and brandished independence as brazenly as bobbed hair after World War I. She gave women freedom to move—to wear pants, pullover sweaters, and flat two-toned shoes. She adapted classic men's sportswear to women in a manner that was entirely feminizing: cashmere sweaters worn with pearls and black hair bows, and jackets cut as comfortably as cardigans. A purist, she preferred natural colors, especially beige, and made jersey, a fabric formerly worn as underwear, the vehicle of her loose-lined couture. The little black dress, sling-back shoes, and the Chanel tweed suit—"in style" for a century—are her legacy. From a sad, impoverished childhood, Chanel became a beacon of café and high society. Her private life was a succession of poignant affairs with aristocrats whose closets she raided for her design. (She closed down her haute couture in 1939, but made a comeback in 1954, at age 71.) Her work and her life, however grand, debunked snobbery with irony. Her lavish costume jewelry—adorned with large and small stones, the semiprecious and the fake—removed the monetary assessment from bijoux and made it something more pure, a thing of beauty.

HER UNIFORM

Tweed suit, pearls, and two-tone pumps

CONTRIBUTIONS

Easy elegance

International style

Sportswear for women

Quilted handbags

Sweater sets

The little black dress

Sling-back shoes

Costume jewelry

Jersey

Kick-pleated skirts

"I am against fashion that doesn't last. I cannot accept th

PRINCIPLES OF DESIGN

"I ask myself why I was launched into this metier, why I became a revolutionary figure in it. It wasn't to put what I liked in fashion. It was, first and foremost, to put out of fashion what I didn't like. I was destiny's tool for a necessary cleansing operation."

FASHION

"Fashion is not something that exists in dresses only. Fashion
has to do with ideas, with the way we live, with
what is happening."

ACCESSORIES

"Perfume is the unseen but unforgettable ultimate fashion
accessory."

COLOR

"Women think about all colors, but not about the absence of
color. I say that black offers everything. White also. They
are of an absolute beauty. Put women in white or in black at a
ball and one sees nothing but them."

FIT

"A suit only looks good when the woman who wears it seems
to have nothing on underneath."

at you throw your clothes away just because it's spring."

The twin set.

In her campaign to give women's clothes an easy elegance, Coco Chanel created the lightweight sweater ensemble that layers a cardigan over a pullover of the same color, in a fine wool or cashmere. The hallmark of propriety and good breeding, typically worn with pearls, the twin set has inherent provocations: it's clingy, with the second-skin look of lingerie, and was synonomous in the Twenties and Thirties with the firm Pringle of Scotland, manufacturer of socks, hosiery, and underwear since 1815. Champagne or flesh colors are classic to it, and its layers suggest the act of undress. Still, the lasting impression is of sporty elegance, a casualness the wearer assumes by instinctively pushing up the sleeves to the elbows. The arms of cardigans can be tied around the waist to hide a bulge, or slung over the shoulders to frame the face with color. They work with jeans as well as in classic combos: with gray flannel trousers or a skirt.

The term "sweater" comes from the heavy blanket that horse trainers would throw over sweating thoroughbreds.

Popularized in the nineteenth century, sweaters were worn for activities that involved exertion, such as sports, which were then exclusively male pursuits. Chanel passed the sweater on to women, it seems clear, from her English lovers' closets full of knit and jersey cardigans.

Bulky knits.

They call attention to themselves in a cheerful, homespun way. They aim for a hand-knitted irregular look, even if the sweater is machine-made. Fashion has become adept at this. Knitters have perfected the art of the exuberant urban knit, still friendly, casual, and chunky, but so inventively patterned and colored as to be sophisticated. The bulk of handknitted charm is tradition, immediately available in the coarse, off-white yarns of the fisherman's knit.

TYPES OF KNIT. Aran: weave associated with the people of the Aran Islands, off the west coast of Ireland. Coarse, handspun wool, usually in a natural off-white color, is knitted in cables, twists, and bobbles down the front and side panels of a sweater, creating an embossed effect. **Fair Isle:** multicolored geometric design, often yoked near the neckline, named after one of the Scottish Shetland Isles where it originated. In the Twenties, the Prince of Wales wore it to play golf. **Argyle:** multicolored diamond pattern in the style of a Scottish tartan, most often stitched on socks.

Sport coats
originated with
manly activity:
hunting, shooting,
or fishing, as
demonstrated by
Ernest Hemingway,
below.

SPORT COATS.

THE ORIGINAL "CASUAL" CLOTHES, SPORT COATS

were the first socially acceptable departure from formal dress. They came relatively late in history—with the Victorian love of country life cultivated by the British aristocracy. True to their function, they tend to be season-specific in fabrics such as corduroy and tweed for fall, linen and seersucker for spring and summer.

Norfolk.
The grandfather of sports clothes, the Norfolk jacket introduced the idea that a jacket and trousers didn't have to match. It takes its name from the shooting parties held on the Duke of Norfolk's estate in the nineteenth century. The Prince of Wales (King George IV), a guest of the Duke, was said to have first com-

missioned the garment from a tailor, stipulating that it should be designed to allow for the easy swing of a gun. Hence, it provides for mobility with box pleats down the back, a band of fabric around the waist, and bellows pockets for carrying cartridges.

Hacking.
The tweed hacking jacket is the most widely worn sports jacket. Side vents and angled flapped pockets were originally designed for sitting in the saddle. It still has a slightly flared skirt and the three-button closure common to all jackets in the Twenties.

Safari.
The safari jacket was devised for the big game hunters of the Twenties who needed a coat that was durable enough to survive in the bush but lightweight enough to take the heat. The original, made by Abercrombie & Fitch, the Manhattan sporting store, along with expedition outfitters Willis & Geiger, used cotton woven three times as densely as standard fabric, and had roomy bellows pockets for essential gear. Ernest Hemingway helped design a model for himself, style number 476, which had an additional pocket on the arm for his eyeglasses.

TIMEPIECES ARE HEIRLOOM ACCES-
SORIES, PASSED ON FROM GENERATION
TO GENERATION. BECAUSE OF THIS
traditional value, as solid as gold, watches have been counterfeited to a zany degree in the last decade. There are copies of copies of copies, to the point where

T I M E P I E C E S

a Swatch Watch—designed as a rubber-banded bit of fun, an escape from the rigors of real jewelry—is itself valued, in certain editions, at the price of great art. All of this frenzy can be avoided with the all-time classics, which come at prices that a pauper as well as a prince can afford. The Timex Mercury, with a round white face and a flex band, was first intro- duced in the Fifties and has never been taken out of production. It cannot even be labeled "retro," as it has always stayed up-to-date—and a bargain.

Cartier watches are a different story: French, evocative of empire and privilege, and the mark of Louis Cartier, who invented the wristwatch at the beginning of the century. The idea of the watch came with the dawn of aviation, prompted by the request of the flamboyant Brazilian aviator and balloonist Alberto Santos-Dumont, who remarked that it was difficult to pull a watch from a waistcoat while manning the controls of a biplane. The Cartier Tank is perhaps the most copied watch in existence.

JEWELRY.

A GOOD STRAND OF PEARLS HAS TRADITIONALLY BEEN THE MARK OF THE GENTLEWOMAN, THE kind men want to marry—but then it depends on how they are worn. They can appear forbiddingly proper, or as decadent as ancient Rome, where they were the rage. The impulse to adorn oneself with trinkets is so primal it has been documented in apes. Ancient Egyptians who couldn't afford real stones wore colored glass instead. Today, jewelry is still split between the nature-given and the man-made. The pitfall of fine jewelry, or fake jewelry posing as fine, is inherent fussiness, obviated by the pearl. It is the most sporting of gems, and the easiest to wear, however weighted with history, myth, and lore. Symbols of love, mercy, and purity, pearls are meant to keep young women chaste and newlyweds from tears. They are never ostentatious, no matter how many strands are worn at once, and look relaxed, age-appropriate, and authentic even when artificial. This accessibility is no doubt due to the pearl's organic nature: The flawed product of the oyster's labor, it speaks to the merely human.

P e a r l s . Most pearls sold today are "cultured," or cultivated by man. They form when an irritant is artificially introduced into a mollusk so that layers of a protective pearly nacre will be secreted around it. They can be round or baroque (irregular in shape). Cultured saltwater pearls, depending on the oysters and waters they grow in, range in color from pinkish-white to yellow and gray. Cultured freshwater pearls are baroque in shape and a dull

Pearls are mysteriously organic: they must be worn in order to keep their lustre and are damaged by perfume.

Pearls have always been considered divine gifts, worthy of royalty.

Before WWI, a pearl necklace was worth the price of an eight-room house.

Faux pearls are made with beads of shell nacre or opalescent glass covered by dissolved fishscale extract or other lustre-inducing substances. Unlike the fakes of yore, they peel like real pearls, and don't break easily.

milky white. Both can be dyed for market. Quality in cultured pearls is determined by a pearl's "orient," or the soft iridescent light from within (created by layers of shell nacre), as well as size, thickness of nacre layers, cleanliness, and color.

Natural pearls form when an irritant enters the mollusk by accident. Once plentiful in South and Central America and the Persian Gulf, natural pearls are now rare, due to overfishing and pollution.

J A C K E T S .
THESE AMERICAN ORIGINALS ASPIRE TO NOTHING MORE

than their adolescent intent: hanging around with style.

Varsity. By popular demand, the archetype of high school and collegiate athletic jackets has shaken off its "retro," frat-house image. Formerly a vintage item stocked in secondhand clothing shops, the varsity jacket is now widely manufactured, and is worn as a contemporary classic. (Brooks Brothers carries a model.) Two-toned color implies a team uniform that can suit up jeans, indoors or out. In a woman's wardrobe, it plays masculine against feminine form in a sensual way that suggests a woman has raided her boyfriend's closet.

Denim. To its great benefit, the jean jacket has never shaken off the brooding, sulky aura of James Dean. Like all Western work wear, it has risen above the law of fashion by being outside it: functional, unaffected, proletariat clothing made for dusty surroundings. Exaggerated proportion has been a recent corruption, with styles ranging from oversize to tight and cropped.

L e a t h e r .

Even the simplest shapes take on rugged glamour in leather. Sensual and primitive, it is a surface on which character writes itself. Rock stars, directors, and anti-heroes through the decades have made the leather jacket a vehicle of macho mystique, alienation, and high drama. Fashion designers created high style out of soft buttery leather. But its lingering appeal is rough and ready. The ordinary car coat, when done in black leather, acquires U-boat connotations, and Mod sleekness. **The Perfecto**—the indestructible biker's jacket worn by Marlon Brando in *The Wild One*—is the classic rebel uniform, made to be beaten up. Designed in 1927 by Schott Bros., it provides bikers with body cover in the event of accident and was distributed directly to them through Harley-Davidson Motorcycles. The thick belt across the back protects the kidneys.

CLASSIC COATS.

TRADITIONAL COATS IN FAMILIAR FABRICS CAN GET AWAY WITH extremes of versatility that other coats can't. Topcoats with velvet collars, for instance, can be worn with jeans as well as black-tie and have been unisex for nearly a century. Basic colors, such as camel and navy, guarantee their flexibility.

The Chesterfield. Originally made for men, it took its name in the 1830s from the 4th Earl of Chesterfield and was adopted by women after World War I. It also comes double-breasted, with pockets, in navy, charcoal gray, or black. Topcoats, of which the Chesterfield is one, are generally lighter than overcoats. In a good fit, the collar of the coat should hug the neck, and the back vent should climb no higher than the top of the thigh. Topcoats need to cover the knee to balance the look of a man-tailored suit.

The Duffle. Devised for the British Royal Navy, the duffle has been an invincibly all-purpose coat since it was sold as surplus after World War II. Designers got their hands on it in the Eighties, throwing hourglass shape into it with heat-molding treatments, and casting it in eye-popping colors. It is rough-and-tumble outdoor wear that can segue to the city—especially if it's cut below the knee.

A SCARF

INVARIABLY PLAYS AGAINST FORM dressing down or up in contrast to whatever it's worn with. The cotton bandanna, for instance, a wildly flashy item on its own, was used by the American cowboy to control dust and, in a jam, conceal identity. A modification of the Spaniard's scarf, it was often the most flamboyant aspect of his workaday wardrobe. The Hermès scarf, made by the renowned French saddlery firm, has become a celebrated classic for the way it combines luxury and sportiness in one fell swoop, printing silk twill with horsey imagery. Because of this self-deflation, it lends itself brilliantly to several common functions—as a belt, the way male tennis players wore it in the Twenties, or, in Grace Kelly's example, as a prescribed sling for an injured arm.

Backpacks. The line from hiking gear to generic carrier has long been crossed by the backpack—good for whatever purpose you put it to. Unisex from its inception, it has no gender issues to contend with. Its only determining feature is fabric. In leather it is certified city apparatus.

Bags. They are extremely personal items into which the patterns of daily life are crammed. They have to be big enough to handle a work load, but not overpowering in proportion. Ease of access and durable construction are crucial and some structure simplifies life, making it possible to find things. Though bright accent coloring is tempting, it should be reserved for the bag that does not get daily use, unless you are a skilled and decided colorist. Brown is a safe option for a day bag—a briefcase or portfolio. For women, a smaller handbag travels more easily into evening if it's black.

"I see a vision of a great rucksack revolution—thousands or even millions of young Americans wandering around with rucksacks."

JACK KEROUAC, *Dharma Bums*

GLASSES.

THE DEFINITIVE IMAGE MAKERS, GLASSES ARE CARICATURES OF character, and yet utterly useful to the point of medical prescription. As the hole in the ozone layer allows more ultraviolet penetration of the atmosphere, sunglasses are becoming less optional for those who spend any time out of doors. (Outdoor light can be twenty-five times brighter than indoors.) This health imperative is a boon to style, clearly delineated in classic frames so charismatic that they have been striking poses for generations: the Le Corbusier, on the intellectual; the Ray Ban, on the Mod; exaggerated Jackie O. frames on the glamorous. With them, mood alteration is as easy as a change of specs; somehow, even the dorkiest classic frames have Clark Kentish sex appeal. In recent years, prescriptive glasses have regained some cosmetic ground lost to contact lenses. Frames are perceived as a personal, sometimes provocative signature.

UVA AND YOU

There are three types of ultraviolet rays: harmless UVC rays; UVB rays—the sunburn rays that can irritate the cornea; and UVA rays, which, over the long term, cause cataracts. In large amounts, infrared rays, or the sun's heat rays, cause retinal burns.

SHOPPING FOR UVA PROTECTION

Sunglasses should transmit only 15 to 35% of available light to the eye. Test them in-store by trying them on and looking for your eyes in a mirror: if you can see them, the lenses are probably too light. Photochromic lenses would be an exception to this rule, as they lighten and darken with sun exposure.

SHOPPING FOR LENS COLOR

The color of lenses determines the way in which they filter out light. **Gray** prevents distortion; colors remain true. **Green** enhances acuity of vision and allows high levels of green-yellow light through to the eye—the light wave to which the eye is most responsive. **Brown** and **brown-amber** absorb blue light, which is refracted in the air on hazy days. They improve contrast and reduce glare.

SHOPPING FOR LENS TYPE

Constant density lenses: good for bright sunshine and glare. **Photochromic lenses:** suited to a variety of conditions, they lighten or darken according to the amount of sunlight. **All-weather photochromic:** for sport. On hazy days they shift from gray to amber to improve contrast and detail. **Mirrored lenses:** glare protection for water or snow sports. **Polarizing lenses:** eliminate direct and reflected glare and are good for driving. Check all lenses for surface distortion: they should be perfectly smooth.

"The future's
so bright, I gotta
wear shades."

TIMBUK3

ACTIVE

The activewear revolution, driven by fabric technology, has forever blurred the boundary between sporting and everyday clothes, and for good reason. Activewear performs. It keeps you dry, warm, cool, and unencumbered in ways that clothes never could until recently. It is worn by astronauts, athletes, and explorers. It is hyper-designed to fulfill a function, not an affectation. Like the T-shirt, its comfort becomes an instant habit. On city streets, the activewear influence is visible in flashes of foul-weather-gear color, and the integration of the high-performance article—a Synchilla polyester top, bicycle shorts, or cross-trainer shoes—into everyday sportswear. Subliminally, it answers a need for wildness, both natural and spiritual. The more complicated life becomes, the more one longs for the great outdoors—even if one's only wilderness experience comes through the Patagonia catalogue.

LAYERING SYSTEMS.

LAYERING IS THE ONLY WAY TO STAY COMFORTABLE DURING PHYSICAL ACTIVITY. THE ENTIRE ACTIVEWEAR WARDROBE, IN ALL ITS BEWILDERING

array of specialized fabrics, is organized around one basic principle: peel off and add layers as needed. Layering has a history. The Eskimos have always done it with furs on the upper body and legs, and the Lapps wrapped thick Norwegian grasses around the feet. The beauty of contemporary activewear is that one can be fully protected from the elements without having to carry the weight of caribou skins, or suffer the chill of condensation from trapped perspiration.

Moisture management is the target of all the technology that has gone into high-performance layering "systems" and their featherweight fabrics. With exertion, the body cools itself through the evaporation of perspiration: it "breathes" sweat. The layers in the activewear wardrobe work in tandem with this cooling system. Like second skins, they enable clothes to keep breathing with the body, instead of saturating the system and impairing insulation as well as ventilation. Hiking boot liners, socks, aerobic leotards, underwear, and ski jackets are, today, all "moisture managers" unto themselves.

HIGH-TECH GLOSSARY. MOISTURE TRANSPORT OR WICKING: dispersal of moisture along a fabric surface away from the body. Fibers are treated to be either hydrophilic (to draw water) or hydrophobic (to repel water). "Push/pull fabrics" do both **WATERPROOF/BREATHABLES:** outer layers that keep out the elements while allowing body moisture to escape **POLYESTER PILE:** insulation layer in fleece, or bunting fabric with "loft" or height for warmth **MICROPOROUS:** outerwear surface of finely woven microfiber that allows vapor to escape but keeps water droplets from entering **THE CHIMNEY EFFECT:** ventilation built into the design of a garment with zippered necks, high collars, open cuffs, and vents that allow hot air to rise and moisture to evaporate **THERMAL INSULATION:** fabrics that keep you cool (such as Coolmax) or warm (such as Thermax), in part by keeping you dry through wicking

**HIGH-
PERFORMANCE
FABRICS**

Capilene (the choice
of NASA's
astronauts),
Thermostat,
Thermax,
NeutraTherm,
polypropylene, MTS,
APT mesh. Some also
have Lycra spandex
for pliancy.

**HIGH-TECH
FUNCTIONS**

To "wick" or draw
moisture away from
the skin. Quick-
drying insulation.

The underwear layer.

How well underwear works depends on its ability to "wick." In damp clothes, body heat is lost twenty-five times faster than usual. Natural fibers such as silk and cotton have wicking ability but do not insulate when wet. A new generation of hollow synthetic fibers—laminated polyester or nylon—transport and disperse moisture more rapidly. They dry out more quickly, weigh half as much as wool, and have the texture of cotton. Underwear weights vary, and should be chosen according to the peak exertion level of a planned activity. The more energy one expends, the lighter the underwear should be.

The insulating layer.

Wool sweaters are nature's great insulators: they do not lose heat retention when wet. They are, however, weighty, slow-drying behemoths compared to polyester pile. Pile, also called fleece or bunting, is breathable, provides warmth with half the weight of wool, insulates when wet, and improves in texture when machine-washed and dried. Pile weights, like underwear, should be chosen according to activity level, and can be worn with other layers or alone. Down is a good insulator when protected by a waterproof shell. It loses warmth when wet.

The outer layer. Protection

from the elements—wind, rain, and snow— is the purpose of the outer layer. Ideally, shells should have pockets and be large enough to accommodate layers underneath. They can work alone or in combination with other layers. Synthetic fabrics offer the most versatility in a shell, and adapt to more varied conditions than natural fibers. Thin shells suit high aerobic activity where breathability is paramount. Non-breathable waterproof shells keep out water but retain perspiration. The most

WASH AND WEAR

Most nylon-based shell fabrics can be washed by machine. Water repellency can be improved by washing in a mild detergent and tumble drying. With age and wear, surface treatments become less effective. A new shell can sometimes be ironed to enhance waxiness and water-beading. Waterproofing spray can be applied to older shells.

HIGH-PERFORMANCE FABRICS

Polyester pile or bunting, with "loft" or height for insulation, such as Synchilla Baby Retro, Retro X, or windproof Synchilla (all by Patagonia), the last of which also comes with stretch Lycra.

HIGH-TECH FUNCTION

Insulation, even when wet. Fast drying, and lightweight.

THIN SHELL FABRICS

For high exertion:
Supplex nylon,
Silmond, Captiva

HIGH-TECH FUNCTION

To allow for maximum
breathability with some
wind- and water-
resistance

**WATERPROOF
BREATHABLES**

Laminates:

Gore-Tex (not a fiber
but a microporous
membrane sandwiched
between the outer shell
and its lining),.
Thintech, or Sympatex

Coatings:

Ultrex, H₂NO, Entrant,
and Helly-Tech

Microweaves:

Super Microft

**Water-repellent
surface finishes:**

Zepel and Durepel

HIGH-TECH FUNCTION

To keep rain and snow
from getting in, while
letting perspiration out

advanced technology has gone into making shells at once waterproof and breathable, and therefore comfortable across a range of activities, from walking to skiing. Born with the invention of the Gore-Tex membrane in the Seventies, waterproof breathables allow moisture vapor to escape while preventing wetness from entering. Coatings and laminates perform this function, along with extremely fine microweaves, such as Super Microft. Surfaces feature a continuous hydrophilic layer to impede contaminates like body oils, detergents, and dirt from clogging pores, and also have a durable water-repellent finish such as Zepel or Durepel to make water bead and roll off.

WATERPROOF VERSUS BREATHABLE.

There is no one fabric or waterproof treatment that can serve every activity, so choose according to need. The more waterproof the fabric, the less breathable; the more breathable, the less waterproof. Walking the dog doesn't require the same high-tech fabric in a shell that skiing does.

A COATING OR A LAMINATE? Both are

effective. However, because coatings have to be applied more thickly to achieve the waterproofing of thin laminates, their breathability rates don't measure up. Laminates tend to be higher in performance and price than coatings. However, they will stiffen in the cold, especially if applied to the garment's exterior instead of its interior.

ENGINEERING FEET.

SNEAKERS ARE NOT WHAT THEY USED TO BE. SHOCK ABSORPTION, 3-D SOLES,

AND SOCK LINERS HAVE CATAPULTED SHOES THAT WERE ONCE AS SIMPLE AS KEDS

into the stratosphere of high-tech. Athletic shoes control "pronation" and "supination"—the inward and outward

roll the foot makes with each step. They reduce mass while they increase cushioning, heel support, and

breathability—all according to the demands of a particular sport. They are machines for the feet into which one

can peer through cut-out uppers and see-through soles. They are the twenty-first-century P.F. Flyers—the sneakers

that showed kids flying in TV ads from the Sixties. You can almost hear their engines revving. With them has

come a new breed of shopper known to salesmen as "shoe dogs": unrelenting consumers who hound them with

well-informed questions about the exact components of the midsole, outsole, and upper. Runners tend to be

shoe dogs, because running and the threat of injury it poses demand the most precision from design. The

technology of running shoes has consequently driven the entire athletic shoe industry, filtering into hiking boots,

lighter-weight "trail runners," "aqua" and boating shoes. As elsewhere in sport, layering is a basic principle: a

supportive inner sock or shoe liner secures a more customized fit atop multiple layers of shock absorption.

SOCKS

Made of Coolmax, with extra padding
at the ball and heel of the foot to
prevent blisters

R u n n i n g   s h o e s . Running demands the most of a shoe: sufficient shock absorption to protect the joints and lower back from injury. The final assessment of a shoe's performance is its fit. New Balance began as an orthotics company and remains the rare running-shoe manufacturer to offer odd, multiple widths. It even makes the double A and the quadruple E, as well as two different shapes of last (one for the flat-footed, the other for the high-arched, and salesmen won't always know the difference). While 95% of athletic shoes are made abroad, 83% of New Balance shoes are made in the U.S.

INSOLE

The glued-in latex insoles of old have been replaced by removable polyurethane inserts that resist moisture absorption and compression. A cavity under the heel of the insole pumps air around the foot with each step. Perforation, from the ball of the foot forward, also assists cooling.

EYELETS

Rustproof aluminium eyelets that resist corrosion from salt water are set in an "oxford vamp," a circular cut of material used on oxford shoes.

LINING

Cotton linings are no longer cemented to the inside of the deck shoe, but stitched to it to abet airflow and moisture evaporation.

OUTSOLE

A low-tech shoe lacks mid-sole technology. The outsole, a molded piece of rubber, is cored out to reduce overall weight. With the toe "bumper" and wrap-around edge, it is baked to the canvas upper in an oven for sixty minutes at 160–180 degrees Fahrenheit.

BOTTOM SOLE

Paul Sperry of Sperry Top-Sider got the idea for a slip-resistant deck shoe when he noticed that the grooves on his dog's paw could get a grip on slippery ice. He cut a similar pattern of slits or "sipes" into the rubber sole of a sneaker. The resulting "Top-Sider" sole was patented in 1936 to squeegee away water as the foot rolls over wet surfaces.

UPPERS

Cotton or leather are classic low-tech materials.

Low-Tech Shoes.

In its simplest form, the all-time classic sneaker is an icon of American ease: footware that can be thrown into a washing machine, that looks good and is carefree. Sneakers first appeared in the 1870s when Charles Goodyear melted or "vulcanized" rubber to canvas shoes as he'd done to mailbags. From this technology came the original Keds. Lately, even the most basic sneaker has acquired a certain sophistication: rustproof eyelets and removable sock liners.

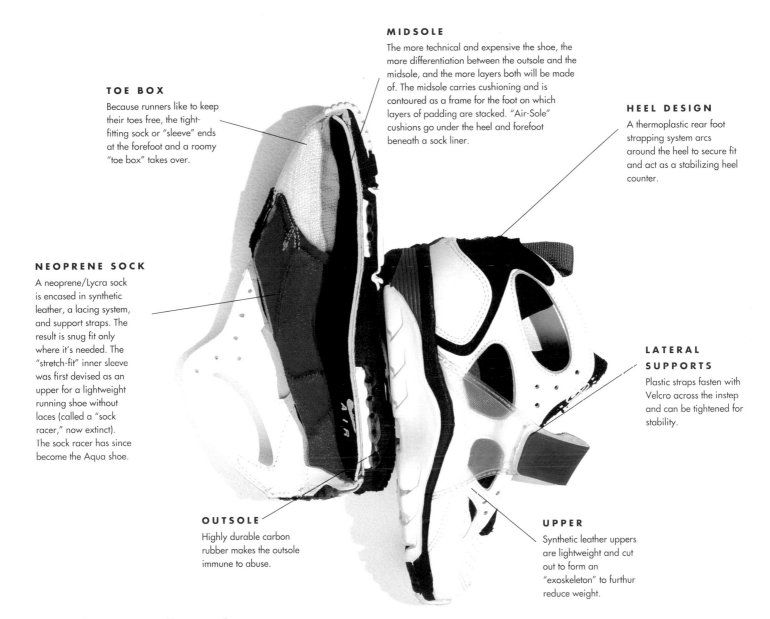

MIDSOLE

The more technical and expensive the shoe, the more differentiation between the outsole and the midsole, and the more layers both will be made of. The midsole carries cushioning and is contoured as a frame for the foot on which layers of padding are stacked. "Air-Sole" cushions go under the heel and forefoot beneath a sock liner.

TOE BOX

Because runners like to keep their toes free, the tight-fitting sock or "sleeve" ends at the forefoot and a roomy "toe box" takes over.

HEEL DESIGN

A thermoplastic rear foot strapping system arcs around the heel to secure fit and act as a stabilizing heel counter.

NEOPRENE SOCK

A neoprene/Lycra sock is encased in synthetic leather, a lacing system, and support straps. The result is snug fit only where it's needed. The "stretch-fit" inner sleeve was first devised as an upper for a lightweight running shoe without laces (called a "sock racer," now extinct). The sock racer has since become the Aqua shoe.

LATERAL SUPPORTS

Plastic straps fasten with Velcro across the instep and can be tightened for stability.

OUTSOLE

Highly durable carbon rubber makes the outsole immune to abuse.

UPPER

Synthetic leather uppers are lightweight and cut out to form an "exoskeleton" to furthur reduce weight.

High-Tech Shoes.

The Air Huarache strips upper sole construction to its bare bones; hence, the "exoskeleton," the synthetic leather exterior with holes cut out of it. The skeleton supplies support where it's needed to create a lightweight trainer with ample cushioning for hard surfaces. Even though it looks complicated, it aspires to the minimalism of the Mexican rubber-soled sandal after which it is named. The Air Huarache has been adapted to cross-training, and court sports such as tennis and basketball.

CROSS-TRAINING.

SINCE FITNESS TRAINING TOOK HOLD IN THE SEVENTIES,

WORK-OUT CLOTHES HAVE BECOME MORE COMFORTABLE

and accommodate the twin goals of cross-training—developing aerobic

endurance as well as muscle tone. Hydrophobic (water-hating) fibers speed

perspiration's progress toward vapor and make breaking a sweat a more

hygienic experience. Wicking is accelerated by mesh linings in shorts and tops.

The fastest-drying fabrics—Coolmax and MicroSupplex—still feel like cotton.

"You don't need to pay athletes to wear your stuff, because

LEOTARD AND LEGGINGS

The high-rise leotard and capri leggings keep pace with "step" and "funk" choreography, in breathable, pliant blends of cotton and Lycra, or Supplex.

DOUBLE-LAYER SHORTS

Doubled-up shorts provide secure cover during aerobic and gym exercise with snug-fitting cotton and Lycra under lightweight cotton jersey.

THE SPORT BRA

A blend of cotton, polyester, and Lycra for fit, lined with Coolmax and Lycra, for comfort.

RUNNING SHORTS

A Coolmax crepe liner accelerates the wicking process in Supplex nylon shorts.

AEROBIC SHOES

Similar to a cross-trainer, an aerobic shoe supplies forefoot cushioning and shock absorption in the heel, along with lateral support to brace the ankle during sideways movement. Lateral supports come as straps over the outside of the shoe, or can be sewn into the construction, often connecting with the lacing system. High-top shoes provide ankle support during "step" and "funk" choreography.

if your stuff is good enough, they have to wear it."

YVON CHOUINARD, *founder and owner of Patagonia*

RIDING CLOTHES.

EQUESTRIAN TRADITION HAS LEFT ITS MARK ON THE MODERN WARDROBE, MUCH OF WHICH IS STILL SHAPED ACCORDING to the ergonomics of sitting in the saddle. The side vents and angled pockets of the hacking jacket, for instance, are poised for horseback. Riding clothes remain elegantly tailored to their task but have the casual style of American Western tradition mixed with the English equestrian. The jodhpurs, boots, and jackets of the English riding habit have long been claimed by fashion and streetwear, however specific their intent and place in a hierarchy of dressage uniform. Jackets made for the motion of jumping have double side vents, while the coat worn in competitive flat ground riding takes only one back vent, as the rider stays, for the most part, seated in the saddle. Breeches must be white for competition though they now come in a range of color. The more expert the equestrian contest, the more formal the dress. "Shadbelly" coats, shaped like cutaways, are worn at high-level competition; "pinks," or red hunt coats, are worn at formal hunts.

GLOVES

Leather for winter, knit and leather for summer

WHITE SHIRT

With a "rat catcher" banded collar

JACKET

An archetype of tailoring tradition, the riding jacket takes one or two vents, depending on whether the rider intends to jump

HAT

The hard riding hat is an elegant crash helmet for the skull.

JODHPURS

Named for the former state in India, jodhpurs have lost their exaggerated flare at the thigh to fit snugly in contemporary stretch fabrics, with suede padding along the inside of the knee and calf for traction.

English

DRESS BOOT

The formal riding boot is in black leather— to the knee.

QUILTED BARBOUR

The traditional quilted Barbour jacket liner provides lightweight insulation and water resistance when worn on its own. Vents accommodate sitting in the saddle.

FLANNEL SHIRT

Layering and water resistance ensure comfort on the trail; this flannel shirt is treated to be water-resistant but is also breathable.

RIDING GLOVES

Leather for winter, knit and leather for summer

PADDOCK BOOTS

Worn for recreational riding, the paddock boot laces to provide adjustable ankle support. It works with breeches, jeans, or jodhpurs. Less expensive than the dress boot, it's a preferred choice for young riders with growing feet. The sole of the authentic riding boot is always sewn, never glued or bonded.

Recreational

RIDING JEANS

English and American riding tradition combine in jean jodhpurs, plied with Lycra. (The most durable jeans are blended with polyester.)

Western

RANCHER'S HAT
The preferred hat of ranchers and cowboys is stiff, durable, and weather-resistant. It's made of fur felt that has been "pounced" (sanded) and greased to give it sheen and water repellency and has a patented sweatband that floats on tape inside the crown to help retain shape.

WESTERN BOOTS. The universal, mythic appeal of this Texan invention is due perhaps to the fact that it was never a fashion to begin with, but a working boot, made for herding and roping cattle from a Western saddle. Every aspect of its design, no matter how fanciful the leatherwork, still serves that purpose. Pointed toes scoot easily into the stirrup; reinforced arches and slanted heels secure the foot when standing up in the saddle. Perfected in the nineteenth century by German bootmakers who flocked to Texas, lured by the romance of the range, the boot has adapted to urban exigencies with the alacrity of blue jeans. Heels have dropped this century to enhance walking comfort. The best cowboy boots, in leathers from anaconda to kangaroo, are still custom-made in Texas with wooden pegs, instead of nails, to secure the sole.

TENNIS SHOES

WARM-UP JACKET

TENNIS SKIRT

POLO SHIRT

SWEATER VEST

SHORTS

Tennis. "Whites" are still regulation attire in this traditional sport. In 1934, standard tennis issue for men consisted of flannel trousers tied with a silk scarf at the waist beneath a polo shirt and blazer: natty but not efficient. Since then, court clothes have become less cumbersome while staying within the bounds of classicism through color. "Whites" deflect the heat of the sun but they also present a psychological advantage: they cast a player as serious no matter how sloppy his game.

G o l f . Curiously for such a conservative sport, wild madras, patchwork, and unmanly colors such as pink are acceptable attire on the green. Golfers modeled the new casual clothes of the Thirties—the Prince of Wales's Fair Isle sweaters and women's pants—and in the Fifties they broke the mold of the gray flannel suit by wearing flashy colors. Lately, golf sweaters treated with a new Gore-Tex for wind protection (not water repellency) have helped extend the season. Golf shoes now have steel spikes with tips in indestructible ceramic tungsten carbide.

S U R F.

SINCE URSULA ANDRESS WALKED OUT OF THE waters of Nassau in the James Bond film *Dr. No* (1962), wearing a wet suit, the sensual appeal of this underwater uniform has been difficult to ignore. Formerly worn by scuba divers or East Coast surfing fanatics, the wet suit's audience has expanded to include anyone, aged six to sixty, who wants to extend their comfort and season in the water. Wet suits are warmer and more supple than they used to be. Neoprene insulation now comes in a "four-way" stretch, laminated with nylon, Lycra, or polyester. But the most dramatic innovation is the use of the metal titanium to raise heat retention by 20%. Woven in "micro flakes" into a suit's lining, it reflects body heat. Surfers report that titanium-flaked suits double their time in very cold water, according to the manufacturer Body Glove.

GLOVES
Essential in cold water

FULL SUIT

SPRING SUIT

TANK SUIT
Shoulder straps and Lycra-blended fabric secure fit in the surf.

SURF TRUNKS
They should be long enough to protect inner thighs from saltwater rash but slim enough not to balloon under water.

SPLIT-TOE BOOTS
Extremities are most susceptible to hypothermia. Windsurfing socks come with and without a contoured big toe to facilitate leverage.

Wet suits were pioneered by Jack O'Neill in the Fifties at Ocean Beach, San Francisco, where the water stays cold year-round. He experimented by wearing Goodwill sweaters in the water, then jackets sprayed with Thompson's Water Seal, and then unicellular foam (PVC).

COMPETITION SWIMSUITS AND GOGGLES

Workout swimsuits should resist degradation from pool chemicals. Tricot knit in nylon and Lycra offers the most durable construction. Suits for competition are paper-thin to stick to the skin when wet, and are worn sized down to eliminate drag.

COMPETITION TOP AND SHORTS

Two-piece suits with partial insulation supply warm-weather waterskiing and windboarding with unconstrained fit in neoprene (rubbery insulation), laminated with nylon and Lycra knit.

"TUBE SUIT"
wet suit with no arms and short legs

"WETTIE"
Australian term for wet suit

"YUMMY YELLOW"
surfer's term for a shark's preferred color of wet suit. Sharks seem to be attracted to bright colors.

from The Surfin'ary: A Dictionary of Surfing Terms and Surfspeak, compiled and edited by Trevor Cralle (Berkeley, California: Ten Speed Press, 1991)

AQUA SHOES. Years ago, Nike experimented with a "sock racer," a stretchy slip-on upper over a rubber sole, to help fleet-footed competitors feel weightless. The sock racer, as such, no longer runs—but it swims, gets wet, and holds feet to waterboards as tenaciously as tentacles in the form of the aqua sock. Its "Dynamic stretch-fit," as

the industry calls this upper design, has been applied to the Air Huarache running shoe (essentially a sock battened into a lacing system). At the beach, aqua socks have forever freed the mind from fear of sharp objects lurking in the sand. Velcro straps add support for surfing and windsurfing competition.

HIKING.

WEIGHT-SAVING TECHNOLOGY IN BOOT

design has increased the agility of hikers and backpackers and brought with it new kinds of trekking. Trail-running, the pursuit at jogging speed of a designated route inspired by the British sport of orienteering, has been spurred on by versatile, lightweight shoes that combine the performance of running shoes with the support of hiking boots. Even heavy-duty expedition boots are now lightweight, with polypropylene shanks replacing steel,

"There is more to

molded to bend where the foot does. The most advanced designs draw on the ski-boot technology of two boots in one: a soft inner boot inside a tough, zip-up outer boot ensures comfort and

minimal break-in time. In order to

avoid blistering, the inner boot keeps

the foot from sliding forward while

walking downhill via polyester mesh

that laces over the arch. Inside, a Clima

Dry insole absorbs thirty times its

weight in moisture and pulls out to

dry overnight. All-terrain shoes

life than increasing your speed."

GANDHI

can scramble, hike, and mountain-

bike with athletic shoe cushioning

atop hiking boot soles, supported by

molded heel-wrapped midsoles and

steel shanks.

BOOT WARMTH

It depends as much on fit as insulation. Blood has to
circulate freely to keep the toes warm. Closed-cell foam provides
the best insulation and the firmest, most responsive fit. Vapor
barrier sock liners (VBLs) in coated nylon keep feet dry when
worn between thin liner socks and outer socks.

SAILORS AND RIVER RATS DO NOT HAVE TO SUFFER SO MUCH FROM the elements with improved wet-weather gear. As kayakers have become more venturesome, paddling jackets and pants have adapted to greater degrees of water immersion and athleticism. Full dry suits extend the season well into winter when worn with insulating layers beneath. Sailors' off-shore boots reduce fatigue with athletic shoe design and removable inner soles.

THE RIVER SANDAL

A breakthrough design in sports shoes, the river sandal has made walking in and around water—in riverbeds or at the beach—comfortable and safe.

All it took was adding an ankle strap to the thong to achieve stability. The invention of Mark Thatcher, a guide on the Colorado River, the sandal was first sold in 1983 to white-water enthusiasts. It's now worn the world over and comes tailored to specific activities. River guides prefer their sandals soled in sure-grip rock-climber's rubber, with snap-buckle strap closures.

S a i l i n g . Heavyweight foul weather gear provides sailors with insulation as well as seam-sealed waterproofing on the high seas. The most rugged resist salt, sun exposure, oil, and gasoline and are made in the manner of an inflatable rubber boat. Neoprene is bonded to finely woven nylon under the pressure of a "calendering" machine. More breathable coatings in foul weather gear include Entrant HP and Vapel, a breathable waterproof membrane. Details build in comfort and safety: hand-warming fleece-lined pockets, non-corroding quick-release hardware, sealed weather flaps, pocket drains, and reflective tape on hoods.

K a y a k i n g . In anticipation of submersion, kayak gear must be water-tight around the neck, wrist, and waist. Jackets have high latex rubber necks and external waistbands of neoprene that lift up to sandwich a kayaker's spray skirt beneath. "High torque" or body twisting athletic paddling is more comfortable in waterproof nylon that is loosened with Lycra. Deep neck gussets allow for ventilation, and high neoprene waistbands on pants can be drawn snugly with an internal cord.

JACKET

A neoprene-calendered shell in oxford nylon with gusseted zippers. The lining is treated for water repellency and urethane-coated to minimize vapor and condensation absorption.

HIGH BIB PANTS

Calendered and reinforced at the knee and seat with Du Pont Cordura, pants are lined with a rugged oxford nylon treated for water repellency.

3/4 FINGER GLOVES

Synthetic leather gloves repel water and last longer than natural leather. Double thickness in the palm prevents rope burns.

OFFSHORE YACHTING BOOTS

Built like running shoes with removable inner soles. Channeled and serrated outsoles can grip a cold wet deck. Nylon drawstring extension cuffs keep them watertight.

PADDLING JACKET

Made of waterproof stretch nylon with zippered mesh pockets to hold essentials.

PADDLING PANTS

Neoprene pants are seam-sealed and contoured to anticipate kneeling and sitting positions.

RIVER SANDALS

Nylon straps arch across the toes instead of securing, thonglike, between them, and neoprene rubber soles are molded for arch support.

FISHING.

A SUBTLE AND ELEGANT SPORT, FISHING FASCINATES ENTHUSIASTS, who are among the most avid and addicted sportsmen around. One of the earliest fly-fishers was a nun, Dame Juliana Berners, who like Sir Izaac Walton, author of *The Compleat Angler* (1653), documented it in its infinite detail. When the sport traveled from England to the Catskills, in New York, it acquired new gear suited to this terrain: waders, for one, helped fishermen who could not, as in England, always find an open bank to perch upon. (The English still don't wade.) Fishing gear has expanded to accommodate all followers of the sport: the bone and deep sea fishermen who congregate in the Caribbean, and the tweedy flycaster given to standing for hours in mountain streams. The multipocketed fishing vest is a recent invention, suited to fly-fishermen's love of gadgetry—the clippers, pokers, and thread cutters they like to have on hand—although a rod, a line, and flies are all that's absolutely required. Non-slip footwear is a strategic concern, as falling in the water is the one real danger that fly-fishermen face, especially when wearing waders that can fill with water. Felt-soled stream boots secure the foot on algae-covered rocks.

"The body and spirit suffer no more sudden visitation than that of losing a big fish, since, after all, there must be some slight transition between life and death."
NORMAN MACLEAN, *A River Runs Through It*

HAT

The canvas duck river hat now provides Gore-Tex waterproofing as well as sun protection. A wire-embedded brim can bend to any shape.

SHIRT

Bonefish Scrubs shirts are made for warm-weather fishing in quick-drying, lightweight Supplex nylon. Supplex has the texture and breathability of cotton but sheds water more readily. Large bellows chest pockets accommodate gear, and discreet styling makes it easy to wear to a restaurant.

FISHING VEST

Made of rugged polyester cotton poplin with its weight evenly distributed by a yoke that extends around the collar. Synthetic fleece fly patches and thirty-three pockets pack utility.

SHORTS

Fishing shorts are made for wading with drain holes at the base of large front pockets that can button over fly boxes.

WADING SHOES

In synthetic leather or quick-drying Cordura nylon, the wading shoe has to provide balance in slippery situations. A toe cap and padded insole make walking on rocks less painful; a non-slip felt sole can be fitted with a detachable stabilizing sole in steel-cleated Vibram to reinforce traction.

BOAT SHOES

Ideal for bonefishing, they provide surefootedness in a lightweight, immersible form. Uppers of water-resistant synthetic leather and porous mesh are edged in soft neoprene around the ankle to avoid chafing. Inner soles of ethyl vinyl acetate foam are removable and drain overnight. Soles squeegee water away underfoot. Overall structure provides more support than an aqua shoe. Brass eyelets are rot-resistant.

CLIMBING.

FOLLOWING ONE LONG ROUTE TO THE TOP OF THE MOUNTAIN

has given way to the high-adrenaline rush of "sport climbing": the pursuit of difficult shorter routes, several of which are completed in a day's outing. Shoe design, as much as equipment, has made tricky gymnastic climbing possible. Unlike the clunky kletter shoes of the Sixties, the new lightweight shoes enhance friction and fit like a very tight glove so that foot and sole move as one against the rock, without slippage. High-cling compositions of sole rubber devised in the early Eighties have spawned methods of foot placement such as "smearing" (securing soft soles to a tiny feature of rock), "edging" the sole to grip a ledge, and "jamming" (inserting and torquing the foot into a crack). Vibram sole technology, now applied to street shoes, was originally developed for climbing and remains fundamental to the sport. Shoes are specialized to "friction," "crack," or "face" climbing. Toeholds are secured by a "slingshot" rand, a rim of rubber that climbs up around the heel, to bring the toe forward under tension. Better-quality shoes have leather uppers and Cambrelle lining.

In Patagonia's latest alpine jackets, aramid, a tough fiber used in tires and bulletproof vests, is combined with Gore-Tex waterproof-breathable technology to create very lightweight, extremely durable gear.

TOP
Cut to lie flat under a harness in cotton and Lycra, with a deep zipper for ventilation

SHOES
Lightweight, medium-flex shoes for steep-face climbing

PANTS
In abrasion-resistant nylon, lined with double-faced cotton, for cool weather

JERSEY
Spandex is sandwiched between two layers of moisture-transporting polyester. The layer next to the skin is more loosely woven to absorb moisture.

GLOVES
Necessary for safety and comfort.

SHORTS
The more panels of fabric sewn into nylon/Lycra shorts, the more comfortable the fit. Seamless chamois pads add comfort.

HELMET
Built to take impact without splitting apart, helmets that have been approved for safety by Snell or ANSI (American National Standards Institute) bear their stickers.

SHOES
A thin, rigid sole secures the foot to the pedal. Rubber outsoles adapt shoes to the rigors of mountain biking.

CYCLING.
BEFORE THE BOOM OF THE SEVENTIES, BIKERS WERE ONLY

dimly visible to the public as fanatics cresting the hills of the Tour de France. As the sport gained popular ground, so did the gear—streamlined, aerodynamically correct, and inherently elegant in a way that acquired urban currency and influenced fashion as far afield as French couture. Lately, the sport has taken on the rough-and-tumble aspects of adventure travel with the advent of the mountain bike.

Clothes are cut to follow the forward lean of the rider: shorts are angled higher in back than in front, sleeves are articulated forward, and outer shells have wet-weather drop tails to keep moisture churned up by spinning spokes off the lower back. Narrow sleeve and neck openings prevent clothes from scooping air. Mountain bikers need extra skin cover to counter the roughness of the trail and have taken to doubling up cycling shorts to protect themselves in a fall, an improvisation which manufacturers have incorporated into mountain shorts that double up on Lycra along the outer thigh. Women can strip shells and jerseys down to high-necked sport tops—long-bodied athletic bras that offer more discreet cover along with ventilation. Brushed inner surfaces on fabrics assist airflow and wicking.

Downhill. From the feet up, the look of the downhill skier has been transformed over the years, driven by the quest for speed and comfort. Lace-up leather boots became foam-injected molds for the feet, equipped with electronic

S K I

heaters. From poplin and woolens in the Sixties came sci-fi shiny plastics in the Seventies, technoid neon in the Eighties, and now a sleight-of-hand "naturalism" based on fabrics that belie their insulating

HIGH-TECH FABRICS FOR UNDERWEAR:

Thermostat

HIGH-TECH FUNCTION:

adjusts to stop-and-start sport

HIGH-TECH FABRICS FOR OUTERWEAR:

Ski Tac, Super Microft, Thermoloft, Thermoloft Plus, Thinsulate, Lite Loft

HIGH-TECH FUNCTION:

water- and wind-resistant, breathable insulation

power and durability with lightweight and refined texture. Jackets that look and feel like chamois are actually breathable, water-resistant microfiber. Bulk has disappeared with the advent of "Thinsulate," one among many light-lined insulators. Thermal under-

I N G

wear, too, has honed in on skiers' needs: Coolmax, a fast-wicking fiber for warm-weather sports, goes into hot spots—under the arm and on the inner thigh—in other-wise insulating, cold-weather underwear.

"Materials have been developed to dry out faster and be more comfortable and lighter. And they really are—even more than fibers and fabrics were ten years ago. It makes it easier for people to get out skiing and that's what's important."

DAVE MENTION,
Manager of Product Research and Testing at L. L. Bean

GLOVES

ETP ("expanded thermal pocket") gloves combine the dexterity of a glove and the warmth of a mitten. Fingers begin at the middle knuckle.

EARWARMERS

Made of bunting

SKI PARKA

A water- and wind-resistant, breathable parka in Ski Tac—a polyamide Tactel microfiber with a luxurious texture

GOGGLES

Double- and triple-lens goggles reduce fogging with a barrier of insulating air between the inner and outer lenses.

JUMPSUIT

In stretch wool

PANTS AND TOP

Loose-lined in Super Microft—a wind- and water-resistant polyester that feels like cotton

Cross-country.

One of the most aerobically demanding sports around, cross-country skiing pushes the limits of fabric technology with requirements for heat dispersal—from sweat and exertion—and insulation against the cold. Form in cross-country clothes has followed Lycra, the speed-demon look of which has added glamour, along with comfort, to the sport. Flexible layering systems include polyester/Lycra underwear,

EXTREMITIES

Fingers and toes are the first to feel the bite of the cold, but most body heat actually escapes from the neck and head. Face masks, balaclavas (hoods), and hats are made to stay dry as well as warm in fast-wicking fabrics such as Thermax, Capilene, and Synchilla pile. Stretch Synchilla balaclavas fit under jacket hoods and roll up off the face into a hat. Long cowls cover the neck completely. Wool provides natural warmth and will absorb moisture but won't lose its insulating capacity when wet. Knit alpine hats now stay drier with interior, fast-wicking headbands. Kayakers wear duckbill caps under their helmets for sun protection, and knit caps in winter.

lighter-weight Polartec pile insulation, and shells and windpants in Supplex nylon that can be shed piecemeal and stowed in a fanny pack. Anoraks and knickers are still classic to cross-country but, like running clothes, have been made far more comfortable, lightweight, and efficient as agents of moisture transportation. Knickers, which provide ventilation when rolled up at the knee, now come in high-tech nylon or fleece bunting.

EARWARMER AND GLOVES

Polartec 200, a double-faced polyester fleece, delivers lightweight breathable protection from the cold in gloves and earwarmers.

ZIPPERED TURTLENECK

A lightweight first layer in fast-wicking polyester and Lycra unzips at the neck for ventilation.

ANORAK

With a traditional shape derived from the Eskimos, the anorak provides rugged lightweight wind protection in two-ply Supplex nylon and can be layered over down or fleece. Underarm zippers and mesh linings improve ventilation.

FLEECE VEST

Polartec Lite—a polyester pile—delivers lightweight, stretchy insulation in a vest that dries quickly.

GAITERS

Often overlooked by novices, gaiters keep snow from soaking socks and pants. They attach to boot laces with brass hooks.

WINDPANTS

Windpants in Supplex nylon protect against snowfall and rain. Worn over long underwear or tights, they have side zippers with stormflaps, and Velcro cuffs.

TIGHTS

An alternative to knickers, tights can work alone or under windpants for warmth.

MIXING

The Essentials

The uniforms of the Nineties are made to be taken apart. Style is all in the mix. Once the strategic choices about color, comfort, and utility have been made, the rest can be left to impulse. Crucial coordinates: the suit with a jacket that can dress up or down at a whim. Jeans, T-shirts, cardigans, and the white shirt travel sartorial miles, fueled by understatement.

"A fashion victim is dressed in des

LEATHER
JACKET

WHITE SHIRT

SUIT PANTS

CARDIGAN
SWEATER

JEANS

SUIT JACKET

SUIT SKIRT

T-SHIRT

igner clothes from top to bottom."

DONNA KARAN

WHAT MAKES A CLASSIC SUIT LOOK AS ORIGINAL AS A FINGERPRINT? MISMATCHING.

Pairing the unexpected. Mixing up genre and gender in clothing, or contrasting textures, projects personal style. When you wear what you like, you will like what you wear. Break apart the elements and explore their limits through combination. The blazer changes personality in partnership: relaxed with jeans; serene in a pantsuit; racy with a skirt and bare clavicles for evening. If a leather jacket functions as your ruby slippers, then let it reinvent itself: wear it with its opposite—a demure skirt—and watch its value double.

ATTITUDE ADJUSTMENT
A T-shirt relaxes a suit.

> "Fashion doesn't come from people who are in it. It originates in the minds of real people."
>
> LAUREN HUTTON

PERSONAL STAMP
Accessories are your imprint.

BARE NIGHTS
Skin dresses the evening.

OPPOSITES ATTRACT
Comfort meets style.

> "The golden rule is that there are no golden rules."
>
> GEORGE BERNARD SHAW

MOOD SWING
Leather for sass, the skirt for class.

"The designers that I have gravitated towards always made simple clothes that you wore, as

Country squire. A jolt of yellow shakes classic riding clothes of their conservatism. The quilted Barbour jacket is an ideal lightweight cover over layers, in the city or country. Black stretch jodhpurs create a sleek, athletic silhouette.

Riding habit. Among clothes that swear allegiance to a way of life, the white shirt stands apart as nonconformist. It sanctions English jodhpurs for everyday use, worn with urban accessories: buckled loafers and a constructed jungle-cat handbag.

opposed to them wearing you. I didn't want to make a statement every time I put something on."

LAUREN BACALL

Fringe element. A single dramatic piece, such as a fringed jacket in red, summons casualness with clout. Riding accessories—paddock boots and gloves—suggest, like a suede vest and white jeans, an easy Western attitude given to flamboyance.

Scarf as skirt. The scarf and the body suit are infinitely versatile and seem to dress up and down simultaneously. As a skimpy evening ensemble the scarf wrapped as a sarong beneath a black tank top appears at once racy and relaxed.

HORSEY SET

Cashmere and jodhpurs

CLASSIC COMBO

Sweater sets and gray
flannels

"Clothes can change moods." GEOFFREY BEENE

KNITS—ESPECIALLY
SWEATER SETS—
HAVE THE GREAT
advantage of hovering between the classic and the sporty. This means you can do with them what you will: dress for a ball or a stroll in the park, if you know how to mine their extremes. Monochromatic color from head to toe heightens drama through radical simplicity. Texture and fabric trigger degree of formality: cashmere on velvet is far richer than cashmere on calvary twill. Color, too, sets tone. Red is bold but has a wide range of application; inherently dramatic, it can be tempered as an accent or raised full volume. Accessories signal that one has positioned a classic either up or down the ladder of formality.

HIGH CASHMERE
Relaxed elegance

151

VOICE OF WISDOM

D o n n a   K a r a n makes "uniforms" that are sensuous, dramatic, and still very easy to wear. She cuts through the chaos of urban life with interchangeable basics, often in black: stretch fabrics, body suits, viscose sarong skirts, pants, and jackets that marry comfort to the dynamism of New York—her city.

More than a designer, Karan considers herself a "doctor" who cosmetically treats anatomical imperfection. Her stretch body suits slenderize and disguise; her stockings cling perfectly. She grew up in the fashion business as the daughter of a Seventh Avenue tailor and model and made her mark in the Seventies as the co-designer, with Louis Dell'Olio, of Anne Klein sportswear. In 1985, she launched her own women's collection, to the acclaim of high-powered women such as Diane Sawyer and Barbra Streisand, who are steady customers. In 1991, she began to introduce coordinated comfort to men with clothes that, even if part of a suit, move through the seasons as interchangeable separates. Like other fashion leaders, she has split her business between designer clothes (called Collection) and affordable basics. DKNY, her "street" collection, sells sportswear essentials—jeans, T-shirts, and accessories. In 1992, she launched a fragrance, "Donna Karan New York," and founded Donna Karan Beauty, the cosmetics division of her company. In 1991, the growing enterprise she runs with her husband, sculptor Stephan Weiss, took in $219 million.

HER UNIFORM
Interchangeable separates in black, cashmere sweaters

CONTRIBUTIONS
Senuous basics
Stretch fabrics
The body suit
White shirts
Stretch skirts
Oversize sweaters
Man-tailored pants

"If a woman is comfortable, she looks great. The

PRINCIPLES OF DESIGN

"I'm designing one wardrobe. Whether you're talking about a sable coat or a pair of jeans, it's one mindset. I don't design anything independently. It's all related—from accessories to hosiery colors. Every product has a reason."

ELEMENTS OF STYLE

"Women and men need a modern system
of clothes that saves time, that makes them look and feel
confident, and pulls it all together."

COMFORT

"How the clothes relate to the body and
how they move with the woman is what's important. Comfort
also means sensuality. That's why I love cashmere. Clothes
should feel wonderful to touch."

COLOR AND SIMPLICITY

"Keeping it simple begins with one color, usually black.
It works day-to-evening. Head-to-toe color also takes the worry
out of the varying length of hemlines."

clothes become hers instead of designer clothes."

The Essentials

Hierarchy and authority are encoded in masculine costume. The more "respectable" the ensemble— as in the matched three-piece suit—the more senior its sensibility. Slight adjustments make the difference. Combining the youthful (blue jeans) with the proper (a vest) rattles conformity until personal style comes tumbling out. Suddenly clothes reveal the man rather than obscure him.

"I've always felt men should use suits not just for business,

"A lot of style is mixing two incongruous elements. When you invest in a good jacket, you wear it with everything from a tie to a pair of shorts."

MICHAEL KORS

VEST

NAVY PANTS

NAVY JACKET

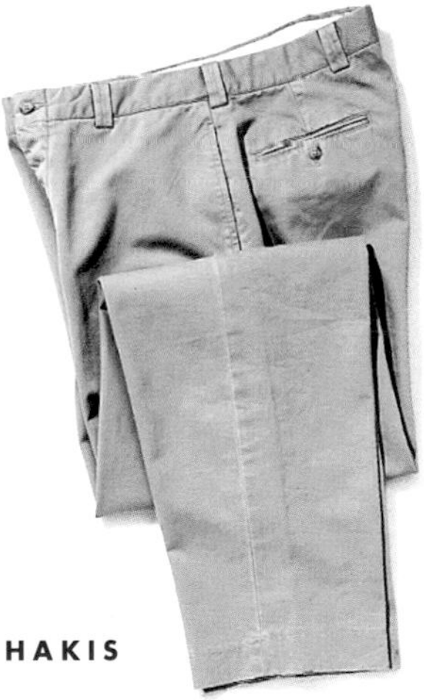

KHAKIS

but as separates that can be worn all the time." JOSEPH ABBOUD

The business suit. The cut of a suit determines its flexibility. An uptight jacket never leaves the office, while a softly constructed suit travels into other contexts. A single-breasted jacket in a three-piece business suit can also unwind over jeans.

Clean cut. The suit jacket sheds years when paired with jeans and a striped shirt. A sweater vest makes the ensemble slightly more weighty— businesslike in a casual office. A shoulder portfolio and loafers remain casually within the bounds of tradition.

The non-suit. A "suit" can be composed of a vest, a denim shirt, and khakis. Dark shirts, especially denim, have new acceptability at the office, with or without a tie. A work bag doesn't have to look like a briefcase; it can be a backpack—in leather.

At ease. Pared down to essentials, the suit acquires a relaxed elegance that suggests socializing. With a white polo shirt, it has the off-duty look of "Friday" dressing, a growing category of on-the-way-to-the-weekend style that tends to go tieless.

THE CARDIGAN CONJURES UP VISIONS OF

armchair comfort, the smell of pipe tobacco, and leather-bound books. Named for the Earl of Cardigan, who led the Charge of the Light Brigade, it has gone beyond classic to become the wardrobe planner's dream garment. It supplants the stiff tailoring of a jacket with the comfort of knit, without sacrificing the idea of ensemble. Versatile to the extreme, it can be casual with jeans, or formal with satin-striped tuxedo trousers. In basic black, it works with virtually any top or bottom, including the skirt. Chanel's genius was to introduce it to women as part of two- or three-piece pairings in the manner of men's attire.

THE CASHMERE CARDIGAN

CASHMERE CASUAL

The cardigan with knit pants and driving gloves

CLASSIC MIX

Gray flannels, cardigan, and silk tie

PAIRED WITH PLAID

The alternative sports jacket

"... buy less, but buy better. In the long run it's cheaper."

JOSEPH ABBOUD

FORMAL EASE

Relaxed black-tie

JAZZ QUARTET

Jeans, leather jacket, cardigan, and T-shirt

FAMILY

INFANT: Comfort
TODDLER: Self-asseration
PRESCHOOL: Experimentation
PRIMARY: Socialization
TEEN: Independence

"Designer clothes worn by
children are like snowsuits worn by adults.
Few can carry it off successfully."

FRAN LEBOWITZ,
author of Social Studies

Clothing a family is a matter of balancing parental guidance with a child's need for self-expression. ✂ Parents have to shop for a moving target— a child's growing body—intent on value for money, easy care, and comfort. Children shop for what they want, for reasons often completely obscure. Parents can avoid a war of wills if they view kids' fixations, however kooky, as mere blips on the scanner of emotional development. ✂ Social survival may in fact hinge on the hideous T-shirt that everyone else wears, and a child's conformity should not be interpreted as insufficient ego. ✂ Identity, from toddlerhood through the teen years, reveals itself through peer bonding, the language of which is often clothes. Amid this surging tide of taste, the best parental influence is empathy.

I n f a n t . At this age, the object is to keep clothes on small squirming bodies from riding up and baring tummies without restricting movement. The layette (the complete bundle of garments, toilet articles, and bedding bought for a newborn) has to include the onesie—the all-cotton body shirt that snaps under the crotch, which is the most efficient design for changing diapers. Known as a "tummy topper," it is highly adaptable to parental preferences of color and pattern. It can look as plain as an undershirt or as jazzy as a party outfit. Also indispensable: the stretchie—100% synthetic (flame-resistant) sleepwear, and one of the most value-packed items in the layette. The "creeper" playsuit, a variation of the stretchie, covers the tummy and buttons up the front. Once a baby starts to crawl, white or pastel colors show too much dirt, and overalls emerge as the answer to urgent sartorial needs for knee protection, secured shoulder straps, and unfettered feet. A single pair of OshKosh B'Gosh bibbed overalls can withstand the pounding of a long succession of crawlers—the more broken-in, the better. If your baby finds them too stiff for comfort, try cotton knit overalls. Extremities need to be covered at this age with flannel-lined corduroy booties, terry-lined socks, and cotton knit hats.

A tip for shopping by catalogue: know an infant's weight in pounds when you order by mail. Land's End and Patagonia catalogues provide an education in shopping for value.

OshKosh B'Gosh was founded in Oshkosh, Wisconsin, in 1895 as a manufacturer of sturdy adult work-wear for railroad men and farmers. It made bib overalls for kids— miniatures of the adult style—in 1900, but the item did not take off until 1962, when it appeared in a national catalogue. By 1990, 95% of its $323 million sales came from children's wear.

T o d d l e r . Clothes for toddlers should promote independence and be designed to be taken off and on easily. This is where parental powers of empathy come into play. At the moment of purchasing a garment, a parent must imagine how a child will make use of it. Can pants be slid on and off without assistance? Is the neck opening of a turtleneck wide enough? Zippers that are stationary and therefore easily pulled open and closed, and Velcro closures on shoes instead of laces contribute to self-sufficiency. Light layers of cotton knit provide more flexible temperature control at school than a bulky sweater. A low sensory threshold—to heat or to fabric texture, including scratchy labels—may effect a child's behavior. Dressing at this age should instill a sense of accomplishment. Avoid defeat by building in options to exercise wilfulness. When an adult offers a choice, a child feels empowered and becomes less contentious. As the mother of a three-year-old boy put it, "I don't have battles. I let him win. Yesterday, he left the house looking like Elton John." A simple detail, such as pockets in which children can carry things themselves, can build a sense of confidence. Delicate shoulder straps, on the contrary, invariably fall down and lead to frustration.

TM & © 1990 WARNER BROS. INC.

© 1990 DC Comics Inc.

VOICE OF WISDOM

A g n è s B . has mined the charm of simplicity for two decades with versatile, utilitarian clothes that remain her own: bohemian, young-spirited, French. What began as a boutique in a former butcher shop in Paris has become an international empire, including twenty-five stores in Japan. She designs with the cool classicism of film noir; simplified suits and pleated skirts have the allure of the *gamine;* and menswear, bought by Robert de Niro, David Lynch, and Harvey Keitel, hints of James Dean and Pablo Picasso. Her cardigan sweatshirt with mother-of-pearl snaps up the front is her best-loved classic, reissued each season in different colors.

At nineteen, as a married mother of twins, Agnès Troublé (her maiden name) began designing what she herself wanted to wear: unconventional, comfortable slips of things you could forget about. Trained at the École des Beaux-Arts to be a museum curator, she instead focused on building a business that was not unlike her life: adaptable to children (she has five, plus four grandchildren). Her cleanly designed stores are geared to family shopping. Children can wear pint-size versions of their mother's snap cardigans, and a "Lolita" line caters to teenagers. A keen art collector, she has opened the Galerie du Jour on the street where her empire began, to exhibit the work of new sculptors, painters, and photographers.

HER UNIFORM

White shirts

Tailored skirts

CONTRIBUTIONS

French bohemian
basics

The snap cardigan

Nautical striped
T-shirts

James Dean jackets

Tailored suits

"Who on earth wants to be a clothes

PRINCIPLES OF DESIGN

"Fashion bores me. Clothes aren't an end in themselves. I think about the most presumptuous thing you can do is define people by what they wear. I feel very strongly that a person's outfit shouldn't suggest wealth or imply any sort of constraint. In fact, that's how I came to be designing clothes. They are for people who'd rather be concentrating on other matters."

PERSONAL STYLE

"I want to see the people who buy my
things using them in their own way to express their own
personalities. A successful outfit is one that gives you pleasure,
and that you don't get tired of."

MIXING

"I like black, white, cream, stripes, flat shoes most of the time
or very high heels and, always, natural looking makeup. I don't
like to be the same woman every day."

CHILDREN'S WEAR

"I design thinking about the pastel colors and hair ribbons I
longed to wear as a child."

horse for some fashion designer?"

"When I see an adolescent who adopts the parents' values 100%, I worry a bit. All adolescents and young adults need to experiment with being different and being themselves."

DR. EUGENE V. BERESIN

"Children are doing their job when they try to connect (through clothes) with their peers."

MARILISE FLUSSER,
*author of Party Shoes to School
and Baseball Caps to Bed*

Early School Years.

The young school-age child dresses for social identification in ways that may sometimes seem absurdly faddish. It is the parents' job to allow for the fickleness of weekly, even daily trends, while providing the kind of overview that is not visible to eyes of this age. All they see are items: party shoes, backpacks, headbands, and hair bows. Being comfortable and looking cool are priorities, and connecting to a group is critical if mystifying to parents. Team sports, and their paraphernalia—baseball caps, league jerseys—become a way for boys to align themselves with admired athletes and each

CAPRICE

Little girls use clothes to express relationship and identity. Alliance with femininity comes through in quixotic tendencies to wear party shoes to camp or in fixations on the color pink.

COMFORT

". . . and another thing I distinctly remember about being a child is that awareness of oneself inside one's clothes. Pinching shoes, a prickling slip, a dress that is tight across the shoulders or around the wrists, ankle socks bunching in the heels of my shoes. Mommy and Daddy never complained of their clothes, but mine seemed a constant torment."

JANE SMILEY, *author of A Thousand Acres*

other. Experimentation runs a gamut of unlikely combinations—girls will wear pants beneath a dress because it makes sense to them as a marriage of style, comfort, and modesty. Girls can become fashion-conscious to a teenybopperish extreme, craving jewelry, especially earrings. Leggings and oversize T-shirts can work as an all-purpose uniform, keeping pace with growing bodies and looking girlish but grown up.

> "All little boys want a superhero shirt. . . . They are striving for identity and see superheroes mastering their environment."
>
> **MARILISE FLUSSER**

SHOES

What's in a shoe? Teenagers can tell. A shoe's shape, style, and brand name represent a morse code of social cues. In high-tech form,
it speaks of athletic feats, physical performance, the power of youth. Shoe subculture includes signals about the tying and color of laces—a fashion statement
that costs almost nothing—and the virtues of the hightop versus the ankle-baring shoe.

Adolescence. The teen years are a time when peer-group identification rules, intensified by raging hormones. At this point, the parental policy has to be for the most part hands-off, as the child knows best what clothing is socially required. "Short of letting them be arrested for vagrancy, parents should let their child choose their clothes," says Marilise Flusser, author of *Party Shoes to School and Baseball Caps to Bed*. The psycho-sartorial line between child and teen is crossed, she maintains, at a precise moment in sixth grade when sex roles usurp platonic friendship. It's a vulnerable passage when teasing about appearance can become merciless. Parental advice can, in some instances, be exercised to ensure age-appropriate style that spares children from premature adulthood. Buying a blazer for a teenage boy can offer lessons in quality and appropriateness while answering the sartorial needs of holidays and formal occasions. For him, a blazer and a pair of chinos looks and feels more comfortable than a grown-up's power suit.

"I believe your style is set when you're a sophomore in high school."

STEVE MARTIN

WHERE

How to shop for simplicity? By focusing on value, whether clothing is luxurious, rudimentary, expensive, or a steal. The costly well-made suit is a bargain, in the end, for the kind of wear it provides, but so is the ten-dollar T-shirt. A Chic Simple store addresses the world beyond its front window. Its clothes fit into the big picture of practicality and comfort, and will work with pieces bought elsewhere. It can have an international vision, but still be rooted in tradition. It can be a cottage industry or global chain; a one-man tailoring operation or a Gap. Once entered, it focuses the mind on what matters.

FREEDOM OF CHOICE
Even as the world shrinks and chain stores expand globally, there are plenty of locales where choice is limited, if there is any choice at all. However, most manufacturers today can aid you in finding a store or even mail direct you. The U.S. numbers below will help give you freedom of choice.

ADIDAS
800/4-ADIDAS
(Casual and sports shoes and apparel)

ANN TAYLOR
800/999-4554
(Clothing and accessories)

ARMANI A/X
212/570-1122
(Giorgio Armani denims and basics)

BANANA REPUBLIC
212/446-3995
(Sportswear for men and women)

BARNEYS NEW YORK
800/777-0087
(Upscale department store)

BASS
800/777-1790
(Shoes)

BENETTON
800/535-4491
(Casualwear)

BIOBOTTOMS
707/778-1948
(Children's clothes)

BIRKENSTOCK
800/487-9255
(Sandals and shoes)

BLOOMINGDALE'S
800/777-4999
(Upscale department store)

BOSOM BUDDIES
914/338-2038
(Nursing bras)

BROOKS BROTHERS
800/444-1613
(Traditional men's, women's, and boys' clothing)

BURBERRYS LTD.
800/284-8480
(Outerwear, raincoats, and knits for men and women)

CALVIN KLEIN
800/223-6808
(Designer clothing for men and women)

CARTIER
800/CARTIER
(Fine jewelry and watches)

CHAMBERS
800/334-9790
(Robes and undergarments in natural fibers)

CHANEL BOUTIQUE
800/550-0005
(Chanel clothes, accessories, and cosmetics)

THE COACH STORE
800/262-2411
(Handbags, leathergoods)

THE COMPANY STORE
800/556-9367
(Sportswear for the entire family)

COUNTRY ROAD AUSTRALIA
201/854-8400
(Tweeds, accessories)

CRAIG TAYLOR
800/879-4500
(Women's shirts in men's cuts)

DAFFY'S
201/902-0800
(Clothing for the family at a discount)

DAYTON HUDSON/ MARSHALL FIELD
800/292-2450
(Men's and women's fashions)

DILLARD'S PARK PLAZA
800/DILLARD
(Upscale department store)

DKNY/DKMEN
800/647-7474
(Fashions for men and women)

DOCKERS
800/DOCKERS
(Khakis and sportswear)

EASTERN MOUNTAIN SPORTS
603/924-6154
(Activewear)

EDDIE BAUER, INC.
800/426-8020
(Outdoor wear and gear)

ERMENEGILDO ZEGNA
212/751-3468
(Designer shoes, clothing, and accessories)

FERRAGAMO
212/838-9470
(Designer clothing and accessories)

FILENE'S
617/357-2601
(Upscale department store)

FREDERICK'S OF HOLLYWOOD
800/323-9525
(Lingerie with sex appeal)

THE GAP
800/GAP STYLE
(Basics for men, women, and children)

GARNET HILL
800/622-6216
(Children's and women's clothes in natural fibers)

GIORGIO ARMANI
201/570-1122
(Designer clothes and suits for men and women)

GUCCI
201/867-8800
(Leather goods, shoes, and bags; men's and women's clothing)

HANNA ANDERSON
800/222-0544
(100% cotton clothing for all ages)

HENRI BENDEL
212/247-1100
(Upscale department store)

HERMES
800/441-4188
(Leather goods and fine jewelry)

H. KAUFFMAN & SONS SADDLERY
212/838-1080
(Riding apparel)

HUSH PUPPIES
800/433-HUSH
(Shoes)

JC PENNEY
800/222-6161
(Clothing for men, women, and children)

J. CREW
800/782-8244
(Sportswear basics for men and women)

JOSEPH ABBOUD
203/869-2212
(Designer clothing)

J. PETERMAN COMPANY'S OWNER'S MANUAL
800/231-7341
(Specialty clothing for men and women)

J PRESS INC.
800/765-7737
(Menswear)

KEDS
212/935-0986
(Shoes and sneakers)

KENNETH COLE SHOES
800/KEN COLE
(Shoes)

LANDS' END
800/356-4444
(Clothes for the whole family)

LAURA ASHLEY
800/367-2000
(Women's clothing and accessories)

LEVI STRAUSS & CO.
800/USA-LEVI
(Denim and sportswear)

THE LIMITED/EXPRESS
614/479-2000
(Sportswear)

L. L. BEAN
800/543-9071
(Outdoor clothes and gear)

LORD & TAYLOR
212/391-3344
(Men's and women's fashions)

LOUIS, BOSTON
800/225-5135
(Classic clothes for men and women)

MACY'S/BULLOCK'S/ AÉROPOSTALE
800/45 MACYS
(Men's and women's fashions)

MILLER STOCKMAN
303/825-5339
(Western wear)

NAUTICA
212/496-0933
(Activewear)

NEIMAN MARCUS
800/937-9146
(Upscale department store)

NIKE
800/250-7590
(Activewear)

NINE WEST
800/260-2227
(Women's shoes)

NORDSTROM
800/285-5800
(Upscale department store)

THE NORTH FACE
800/719-NORTH
(Outdoor wear and equipment)

OLIVER PEOPLES
310/657-5475
(Eyeglasses and accessories)

ONE 212
800/216-2221
(Fashionable basics, accessories, shoes)

ORVIS
800/541-3541
(Outerwear)

PARISIAN
205/940-4000
(Upscale department store)

PATAGONIA
800/336-9090
(Activewear)

PENDLETON WOOLEN MILLS
212/661-1709
(Men's and women's outerwear)

POLO/RALPH LAUREN
212/606-2100
(Designer clothes for men, women, and children)

PRODUCT
800/89-PRODUCT
(Designer specialty store)

RAGS
914/967-4144
(Contemporary women's fashions)

REI
800/426-4840
(Activewear and recreational equipment)

REMO (AUSTRALIA)
2/331-5007
inforemo@remo.com.au
(Classic clothing and accessories)

RICH'S
404/913-4000
(Better women's merchandise)

THE RIGHT START CATALOG
800/526-5220
(Children's clothes)

ROBY'S INTIMATES
800/878-8BRA
(Bras)

SAKS FIFTH AVENUE
212/753-4000
(Upscale department store)

SLATES
800/SLATES-1
(Men's dress pants)

SPEEDO
800/5-SPEEDO
(Swimwear and sportswear)

SPIEGEL
800/345-4500
(Coats, lingerie, accessories, and clothes)

THE SPORTS AUTHORITY
954/735-1701
(Sports apparel)

STERNS
800/624-4048
(Men's and women's clothes and accessories)

STUSSY
212/274-8855
(Unisex and men's sportswear)

**THE SUNGLASS HUT
INTERNATIONAL, INC.**
800/597-5005
*(Sunglasses, all-purpose eyewear, and sports
brands)*

TALBOTS
800/825-2687
*(Clothing and accessories for women and
children)*

TARGET STORES
800/800-8800
(Discounted designer apparel)

THOR-LO
800/438-0286
(Socks)

TIFFANY & CO.
212/605-4612
(Fine jewelry and accessories)

TIMBERLAND
800/258-0855
(Outdoor shoes, boots, and activewear)

TJ MAXX
800/926-6299
(Discounted clothing and accessories)

TOMMY HILFIGER
212/840-8888
(Men's and women's activewear)

TSE
212/472-7790
(Cashmere clothing)

TWEEDS
800/999-7997
(Basics, accessories, shoes)

URBAN OUTFITTERS
215/569-3131
(Sportswear basics)

VICTORIA'S SECRET
800/888-8200 For catalog
(Intimate apparel)

WATHNE
800/942-1166
*(Clothing and accessories for men and
women)*

WOOLRICH
800/995-1299
(Casual and outdoor wear)

NATIONAL LISTINGS

CALIFORNIA

GREAT PACIFIC IRON WORKS
235 West Santa Clara Street
Ventura, CA 93001
805/643-6075
(Activewear)

L.A. EYE WORKS
7407 Melrose Avenue
Los Angeles, CA 90046
213/653-8255
(Eyeglass frames)

LEATHERS & TREASURES
7623 Beverly Boulevard
Los Angeles, CA 90036
213/655-7541
(Specialty leathers)

MAXFIELD
8825 Melrose Avenue
Los Angeles, CA 90069
310/274-8800
*(European and Japanese designer clothes for
men and women)*

REAL CHEAP SPORTS
36 West Santa Clara Street
Ventura, CA 93001
805/648-3803
(Discounted activewear)

**RON HERMAN/FRED SEGAL
MELROSE**
8100 Melrose Avenue
Los Angeles, CA 90046
213/651-3342
(Department store)

WILKES BASHFORD
375 Sutter Street
San Francisco, CA 94108
415/986-4380
(Luxury menswear)

DISTRICT OF
COLUMBIA

BETSY FISHER
124 Connecticut Avenue, NW
Washington, DC 20036
202/785-1975
(Discounted designer apparel)

BRITCHES OF GEORGETOWN
1225 Wisconsin Avenue, NW
Washington, DC 20007
202/333-3666
(Affordable classics for men and women)

GEORGIA

**SUMMERVILLE RAGS
AND CLASSICS**
1502 Monte Sano Avenue
Augusta, GA 30904
706/738-4884
(Classic women's clothes and accessories)

ILLINOIS

BIGSBY & KRUTHERS
1750 North Clark Avenue
Chicago, IL 60614
312/440-1750
(Menswear)

THE KNOT SHOP
57 West Grand Avenue
Chicago, IL 60610
312/664-5668
(Ties and accessories for men)

ULTIMO
114 East Oak Street
Chicago, IL 60611
312/787-0906
(Designer clothes for men and women)

NEW MEXICO

SANBUSCO
550 Montezuma Avenue
Santa Fe, NM 87501
505/988-1664
(Southwestern and contemporary menswear)

NEW YORK

AGNES B.
116 Prince Street
New York, NY 10012
212/925-4649
(Clothes for men, women, and children)

BARRY KIESELSTEIN-CORD
5 East 57th Street
New York, NY 10022
212/754-6388
(Women's fashions and accessories)

BERGDORF GOODMAN
754 Fifth Avenue
New York, NY 10019
212/753-7300
(Upscale department store)

BEST OF SCOTLAND
581 Fifth Avenue
New York, NY 10017
212/644-0403
(Women's cashmere sweaters at discount)

**BILLY MARTIN'S WESTERN
WEAR, INC.**
812 Madison Avenue
New York, NY 10021
212/861-3100
(Western wear and boots)

BRIAN BUBB
38 West 21st Street
New York, NY 10010
212/206-7124
(Neckties, menswear)

BUFFALO CHIPS
116 Greene Street
New York, NY 10012
212/274-0651
(Southwestern clothes and boots)

CANAL JEAN
504 Broadway
New York, NY 10012
212/226-1130
(Casual and vintage clothes)

CENTURY 21
22 Cortland Street
New York, NY 10007
212/227-9092
(Discounted men's and women's clothes)

C. P. COMPANY
175 Fifth Avenue
New York, NY 10010
212/260-1990
(Italian sportswear)

DOLLAR BILL
99 East 42nd Street
New York, NY 10017
212/867-0212
(Discounted men's and women's clothes)

FELISSIMO
10 West 56th Street
New York, NY 10019
212/956-4438
*(Environmentally conscious men's and
women's clothes)*

JACADI
1281 Madison Avenue
New York, NY 10128
212/369-1616
*(Classic, well-priced children's clothes,
ages 3 to 12 years)*

J. M. WESTON
42 East 57th Street
New York, NY 10022
212/308-5655
(Classic shoes for men)

MARAOLO SHOE FACTORY OUTLET
131 West 72nd Street
New York, NY 10023
212/787-6550
*(Makers of Giorgio Armani,
Donna Karan, and DKNY shoes)*

**THE METROPOLITAN
MUSEUM OF ART**
1000 Fifth Avenue
New York, NY 10028
718/326-7050
(Copies of period jewelry, scarves, neckties)

MIKIMOTO AMERICA CO, LTD.
730 Fifth Avenue
New York, NY 10017
212/586-7153
(Pearls)

MILLER HARNESS CO.
117 East 24th Street
New York, NY 10010
212/673-1400
(Riding apparel)

**MORGENTHAL FREDERICS
OPTICIANS**
944 Madison Avenue
New York, NY 10021
212/744-9444
(Designer eyeglasses)

**MUSEUM OF MODERN ART
DESIGN STORE**
44 West 53rd Street
New York, NY 10019
212/767-1050
(Jewelry and leather accessories)

NEW REPUBLIC
93 Spring Street
New York, NY 10012
212/219-3005
(Classic menswear)

**NORIKO MAEDA BOUTIQUE
AT THE CARLYLE**
985 Madison Avenue
New York, NY 10021
212/717-0330
(Women's fashions and accessories)

**PARAGON SPORTING
GOODS**
867 Broadway
New York, NY 10003
212/255-8036
(Activewear)

PAUL SMITH
108 Fifth Avenue
New York, NY 10011
212/627-9770
*(Men's suits, sportswear, and
furnishings)*

PAUL STUART
Madison Avenue at 45th Street
New York, NY 10017
212/682-0320
(Classic menswear, some womenswear)

PENDLETON SHOPS
489 Fifth Avenue, 25th floor
New York, NY 10022
212/661-0655
(Sportswear for men and women)

ROBERT LEE MORRIS
456 West Broadway
New York, NY 10012
212/673-2000
(Contemporary artisanal jewelry)

THE SHIRT STORE
51 East 44th Street
New York, NY 10017
212/557-8040
(Men's shirts)

SMALL CHANGE
964 Lexington Avenue
New York, NY 10021
212/772-6455
(Clothes for children and infants)

SULKA & CO.
430 Park Avenue
New York, NY 10022
212/980-5200
*(Classic, luxury menswear, coats,
loungewear, and accessories)*

TED MUEHLING SHOP
47 Greene Street
New York, NY 10013
212/431-3825
(Contemporary artisanal jewelry)

WORTH & WORTH
331 Madison Avenue
New York, NY 10017
212/867-6058
(Men's hats)

P E N N S Y L V A N I A

HECHT'S
1300 Market Street
Philadelphia, PA 19107
215/422-2000
(Men's and women's fashions)

WAYNE EDWARDS
1521 Walnut Street
Philadelphia, PA 19102
215/563-6801
(Designer menswear)

WISCONSIN

OLSON'S MILL DIRECT
1641 South Main Street
Oshkosh, WI 54901
414/426-6360
*(Discounted OshKosh B'Gosh children's
clothes)*

**INTERNATIONAL
LISTINGS**

AUSTRIA

EDUARD KETTNER
Postfach 1
2334 Vosendorf Sud
Vienna
1/691-6410
(Outdoor wear)

AUSTRALIA

Melbourne

BETTINA LIANO
150 Chapel Street
South Varra
3/827-0063
(Basics)

DAIMARU
21 La Trobe Street
3/660-6666
(Upscale department store)

GEORGES
162 Collins Street
3/283-5535
(Upscale department store)

**STEPHEN DAVIES
DESIGNER SHOES**
65 Gertrude Street
Fitzroy
3/419-6296
(Custom-made shoes)

Sydney

BELINDA
8 Transvaal Avenue
Doubleday
2/328-6288
(Australian designer clothes)

COUNTRY ROAD
142 Pitt Street
Pitt Street Mall
2/282-6299
(Classic sportswear)

DAVID JONES
Elizabeth Street
2/266-5544
(Upscale department store)

DINOSAUR DESIGNS
339 Oxford Street
Paddington
2/361-3776
(Jewelry made from natural materials)

MORRISSEY & EDMISTON
Strand Arcade
Pitt Street Mall
2/232-7606
*(Moderately priced fashions for men and
women)*

CANADA

Montreal

OGILVY
1307 rue Sainte-Catherine Ouest
514/842-7711
*(Traditional tweeds for men, smock
dresses for little girls)*

Toronto

ATOMIC AGE
350 Queen Street West
416/ 977-1296
(Designer clothes from Canadian designers)

LA MODE DE VIJA
601 Markham Street
Mirvish Village
416/360-6540
(Discount designer clothing)

SPORTABLES
Queens Quay Terminal
416/360-6450
(Casualwear in natural fibers)

DENMARK

BRUNO JOEL
Nyostergade 3
Copenhagen
33/156-508
(Shoes)

GEORG JENSEN
Amagertorv 4
1160 Copenhagen
33/114-080
(Jewelry)

GERDA LYNGGAARD
Østergade 15
1100 Copenhagen
33/124-712
(Jewelry)

ILLUM
Østergade 52
1100 Copenhagen K
33/144-002
(Upscale department store)

MAGASIN DU NORD
Kongens Nytorv 13
1050 Copenhagen K
33/114-433
(Upscale department store)

MULBERRY
Østergade 13
1100 Copenhagen
33/327-520
(Classics)

NORGAARD
Amagertorv 13, 2nd floor
1160 Copenhagen
33/122-428
(Danish casualwear)

F R A N C E

Paris

AGNES B.
3-6 rue du Jour, 1er
0140/03-45-00
(Suits, leathers, and knit basics for men, women, children, and teens)

A.P.C
4-7 rue Fleurus, 6^{e}
0145/48-65-29
(Tailored clothes for men and women)

AU PRINTEMPS
64 Boulevard Haussmann, 9^{e}
0142/82-50-00
(Department store)

BONPOINT
15 rue Royale, 8^{e}
0147/42-52-63
(Classic infants' and children's clothes)

CHARVET
28 Place Vendome, 1er
0142/60-30-70
(Men's shirts made to order, accessories)

CLEMENTINE
101 rue de Seine, 6^{e}
0143/26-64-80
(Classic women's clothes made to order)

CRISTIANI
2 rue de la Paix, 2^{e}
0142/61-12-34
(Expert tailoring)

GALERIES LAFAYETTE
40 Boulevard Haussmann, 9^{e}
0142/82-34-56
(Department store)

HEMISPHERES
1 Boulevard Emile-Augier, 16^{e}
0145/20-13-75
(Traditional sportswear for men and women)

HERMÈS
24 rue du Faubourg Saint-Honoré, 2^{e}
0140/17-47-17
(Men's and women's clothes, fine leather bags, accessories, printed silk scarves, and jewelry)

IL POUR L'HOMME
209 rue Saint-Honoré, 1er
0142/60-43-56
(Menswear and accessories)

INÈS DE LA FRESSANGE
14 Avenue Montaigne, 8^{e}
0147/23-64-87
(Clothing, accessories, jewelry, and luggage from the former star model of Chanel)

JACADI
7 rue Gustave-Courbet, 16^{e}
0145/53-33-73
(Classic, children's clothes, ages 3 to 12 years)

POUPIE CADOLLE
14 rue Cambon, 1er
0142/60-94-94
(Made-to-measure undergarments)

PRINCESSE TAM-TAM
23 rue de Grenelle, 7^{e}
0145/49-28-73
(Cotton lingerie and boyish pajamas)

RECIPROQUE
95 rue de la Pompe, 16^{e}
0147/04-30-28
(Secondhand designer women's fashions, bags, and costume jewelry)

RENAUD PELLEGRINO
10 rue Saint Roch, 1er
0142/60-69-36
(Fine leather handbags)

ROBERT CLERGERIE
5 rue du Cherche-Midi, 6^{e}
0145/48-75-47
(Shoes for women inspired by classic men's styles)

SABBIA ROSA
73 rue des Saints-Pères, 6^e
0145/48-88-37
(Classic lingerie)

SCOOTER
10 rue de Turbigo, 1er
0145/08-89-31
*(Costume and ethnic jewelry, bags, and
clothes for young women)*

SOMMIER
3 Passage Brady, 10^e
0142/08-27-01
(Designer clothes at discount)

SULKA & CO.
2 rue de Castiglione, 1er
0142/60-38-08
*(Classic, luxury men's fashions and
accessories)*

UPLA
22 rue de Grenelle, 7^e
0140/26-49-96
*(Handbags inspired by traditional
hunting and fishing bags)*

GERMANY

Berlin

DURCHBRUCH
Schluterstrasse 58
30/881-5568
(Women's fashions)

E. BRAUN AND COMPANY
Kurfurstendamm 43
30/881-3462
(Designer clothes)

HALLHUBER
Kurfurstendamm
30/883-1248
(Basics)

HORN
Kurfurstendamm 213
30/881-4055
(Second-line designer clothes)

KADEWE
Taventzienstrasse 21-24
30/218-1028
(Department store for basics)

KRAMBERG
Kurfurstendamm 56-57
30/323-6058
(Designer clothes)

NARDINI
Schluterstrasse 70
30/316-464
(Moderately priced clothes for women)

SELBACH
Kurfurstendamm 195/196
30/883-2526
(Men's fashions)

Hamburg

JIL SANDER
Milchstrasse 13
2000
40/553-02173
(Simple designer women's fashions)

Munich

LUDWIG BECK
Marienplatz 11
89/236-910
(Upscale department store)

MAENDLER
Theatinerstrasse 7
89/291-3322
(Classics)

MEY & EDLICH
Theatinerstrasse 7
89/290-0590
(Upscale department store)

PATAGONIA
Leopoldstrafe 47
89/399-299
(Activewear)

PAYDAY
Ainmillerstrasse 2
89/336-550
(Basics)

THERESA
Theatinerstrasse 31
89/224-845
(Designer clothes)

GREAT BRITAIN

London

BROWNS
23-27 South Molton Street, W1Y IDA
171/491-7833
*(Specialty store for men and women,
showcasing leading designers)*

BURBERRYS LTD.
165 Regent Street, W1R 8PH
171/734-4060
*(Raincoats, outerwear, and sportswear for
men and women)*

BUTLER & WILSON
189 Fulham Road, SW3
171/352-3045
(Costume jewelry)

ELIZABETH GAGE
20 Albemarle Street, W1X 4LE
171/499-2879
(Fine gold jewelry)

**HACKETTS GENTLEMAN'S
CLOTHIERS**
138 Sloane Street, SW1 X9AY
171/730-3331
(Classic English menswear)

HARVEY NICHOLS & CO. LTD.
109-125 Knightsbridge, SW1X 7RJ
171/235-5000
(Upscale department store)

H. HUNTSMAN & SONS LTD.
11 Savile Row, W1
171/734-7441
(Suits made to order)

JEAN MUIR ESSENTIALS
109-125 Knightsbridge, SW1
171/235 5000
(Minimalist basics for women)

JOHN LOBB
9 Saint James's Street, SW1
171/930-3664
(Custom-made shoes and boots for men)

JOSEPH
23 Brompton Arcade, SW1
171/584-1857
(Patterned knits for women)

LIBERTY PLC
210-220 Regent Street, W1R 6AH
171/584-1857
(Patterned knits for women)

THE LIBRARY
268 Brompton Road, SW3 2AS
171/589-6569
(Men's fashions, accessories, and books)

MARKS & SPENCER PLC
113 Kensington High Street, W8
171/938-3711
(Department store)

MUJI NO BRAND GOODS
39 Shelton Street, WC2
171/379-1331
*(Generic clothes made from natural fibers in
basic colors)*

N. PEAL & CO. LTD.
37 Old Burlington Arcade, W1
171/493-5378
(Cashmere sweaters for women)

PAUL SMITH
41-44 Floral Street, WC2E 9DG
171/379-7133
(Menswear)

PETER JONES
Sloane Square, SW1
171/730-3434
(Department store)

SULKA & CO.
19 Old Bond Street, W1X 3DA
171/493-4468
*(Classic, luxury menswear, coats,
loungewear, and accessories)*

**SWAINE, ADENEY, BRIGGS &
SONS LTD.**
185 Picadilly, W1
171/734-4277
*(Riding clothes, tweed sportscoats, classic
English sweaters, men's hats, and
umbrellas)*

I T A L Y

Milan

ERMENEGILDO ZEGNA
via Pietro Verri, 3
2/795521
(Men's clothing)

ETRO
via Montenapoleone, 5
2/550201
*(Ties, scarves in paisley silks and cashmere,
men's and women's fashions, and leather
goods)*

GIORGIO ARMANI
via Sant' Andrea, 9
2/76-02-27-57
(Designer clothes for men and women)

IL SALVAGENTE
via Fratelli Bronzetti, 16
2/742-6642
(Discount designer stock house)

LA RINASCENTE
Piazza Duomo
2/72-00-22-10
(Department store)

NAVIGLI FLEA MARKET
Mercato Papiniano
Viale Papiniano, from Porta Ticinese to
Porta Genova
*(Knits, cashmere sweaters, and casual
clothes)*

NN STUDIO
Corso Como, 10
2/659-0266
(Modern classics for men and women)

OFELIA
Corso Matteotti, 10
2/33-60-33-36
(Made-to-measure undergarments)

PELLINI BIJOUX
via Morigi, 9
2/72-01-02-13
(Fine jewelry by Donatella Pellini)

PRADA
Galleria Vittorio Emanuele 63-65
and Via della Spiga, 1
2/760-8636
(Fine shoes, bags, and leather accessories)

PUPI SOLARI
Piazza Tommaseo, 3
2/463-325
(Children's clothes)

SEBASTIAN
via Borgospesso, 18
2/780-532
(Custom-made shoes)

ZORAN
Corso Matteoti, 1A
2/76-00-79-58
(Simple, luxurious women's clothes)

Rome

ALBERTELLI
via dei Prefetti, 11
6/6873401
(Quality shirts, basics for men)

BALLOON
Piazza di Spagna, 35
6/678-0110
(Discounted basics)

**LE TARTARUGHE AND
COMPANY**
via Pie di Marmo, 29
6/684-0517
(Classics)

MAS
Piazza Vittorio Emanuele
6/446-9010
(Discount shopping, bargain cashmere)

JAPAN

Osaka

**FELISSIMO'S MAIL ORDER
CATALOGUE**
1-1-8 Shinsenri-Mishimachi
Toyonaka-Shi, Osaka 565
6/934-0321
*(Environmentally conscious apparel for men
and women)*

Tokyo

ISETAN
3-14-1 Shinjuku
Shinjuku-ku
3/3352-1111
*(Department store carrying Japanese,
European, and American designers)*

JURGEN LEHL
5-3-10 Minamiaoyama
Minato-ku
3/3498-6723
*(Clothes and textiles developed by Japanese
designers)*

MATSUDA
3-16-9 Minamiaoyama
Minato-ku
3/3478-0998
*(Clothes that combine Western and Japanese
sensibilities)*

MIKIMOTO
4-5-5 Ginza
Chuo-ku
3/3535-4611
(Pearls)

MITSUKOSHI
1-4-1 Muromachi
Nihombashi, Chuo-ku
3/3241-3311
*(Department store carrying Western
designers and traditional Japanese goods)*

MUJIRUSHI RYOHIN
4-22-8 Taishido
Setagaya-ku
3/3241-3311
*(Generic clothes made from natural fibers in
basic colors)*

TAKASHIMAYA
2-4-1 Nihonbashi
Chuo-ku
3/3211-4111
*(Japanese and Western designer goods,
kimonos)*

TASAKI PEARL GALLERY
1-3-3 Akasaka
Minato-ku
3/5561-8881
(Pearls)

NORWAY

Oslo

NINO
Karl Johansgate 25
2/424-495
(Scandinavian-designed clothes)

PALEET
Karl Johansgate 37-44
2/423-501
(Shopping center for basics)

STEEN & STRÖM
Kongcnsgate 23
2/416-800
(Upscale department store)

SPAIN

Barcelona

GROC
Rambla de Catalonia, 100
3/215-7778
(Classic clothing)

JEAN-PIERRE BUA
Diagonal 469
3/439-7100
(Designer boutique)

Madrid

ADOLFO DOMINGUEZ
Calle Serrano, 96
1/576-7053
(Designer clothes for men and women)

CORTE INGLES
Raimundo Fernandez Villaverde, 79
1/532-8100
(Upscale department store)

LOEWE
Calle Serrano, 26
1/435-0645
(Luxury leather goods)

!OH QUE LUNA!
Calle Ayala, 32
1/431-3725
(Lingerie, sleepwear)

SYBILLA
Calle Jorge Juan, 12
1/578 1322
(Modern, romantic designer clothes)

ZARA
Grande Ville, 32
1/407-1300
(Sportswear basics)

SWEDEN

Stockholm

CHAMPAGNE
Hamngatan 10
8/20-9005
(Knitwear)

ERIKSSON & HAMNGATAN
Nybrogatan 20
8/663-2610
(Knitwear)

GUL & BLA HAMNGATAN
Hamngatan 10
8/611-2850
(Swedish-designed clothing)

MARC O'POLO
Biblioteksgatan 11
8/611-0504
(Jeans and sweaters)

MATHILDE
Biblioteksgatan 12
8/611-9810
(Quality basics)

MULBERRY
Birger Jarlsgatan 10
8/611-4688
(Classic, casual clothes)

NK
Hamngatan 18-20
8/762-8000
(Upscale department store)

PEAK PERFORMANCE
Jacobbergsgatan 6
8/611-3400
(Outdoor clothes)

RESOURCES

BASICS

28–29 **BOXERS** - Brooks Brothers; **BRIEFS** - Jockey

30–31 **BLACK COTTON BRA** - Hanro; **BLACK LACE BUSTIER** - Barney's New York; **BLACK CAMISOLE** - Hanro; **CONTROL PANTIES** - Wacoal

32–33 **SOCKS** - (from left) Cole Haan, Gold Toe, Cole Haan; **HOSIERY** Polo/Ralph Lauren

34–35 **MEN'S SHOE** - Johnston & Murphy; **PUMP** - Chanel

36–37 **LOAFERS** - Brooks Brothers, Timberland; **BALLET FLAT** - Chanel

38–39 **WHITE T-SHIRT** - The Gap; **T-SHIRTS** - Barney's New York

43 **WHITE SHIRT** - Brooks Brothers

44–45 **SHIRT COLLARS & CUFFS** - Bergdorf Goodman Men

47 **DENIM SHIRT** - The Gap

48–49 **CASHMERE TURTLE NECK** - Malo Tricot; **NAVY SWEATER** - Brooks Brothers; **SMEDLEY POLO SHIRT** - Bergdorf Goodman Men

51 **JEANS** - Levis

54–55 **GRAY PANTS** - Alan Flusser; **KHAKIS** - Polo/Ralph Lauren

63 **TUXEDO** - Giorgio Armani

65 **COAT** - Burberry's of London

STYLE

75 **SPORT COAT** - Alan Flusser

OPTIONS

83 **STRIPED SHIRTS** - Brooks Brothers

84 **BELTS** - Joseph Abboud (braided); Polo/Ralph Lauren

85 **TIE** - Donna Karan Men

86 **SUSPENDERS** - Polo/Ralph Lauren

87 **VEST** - Polo/Ralph Lauren

88–89 **VARSITY JACKET** - Brooks Brothers; **DENIM JACKET** - Levis; **LEATHER COAT** - New Republic; **LEATHER MOTORCYCLE JACKET** - Perfecto; Canal Jeans

90 **RED SWEATER SET** - TSE Cashmere

91 **IVORY CABLE SWEATER** - DKNY

95 **WATCHES** - Timex; Cartier

96 **PEARLS** - CIRO

100–1 **CHESTERFIELD** - Polo/Ralph Lauren; **DUFFLE COAT** - Brooks Brothers

103 **BANDANNA** - Canal Jeans; **SILK SCARVES** - Hermès

104–5 **BACK PACK** - Coach; **SATCHEL** - Cole Haan; **HERMÈS KELLY BAG** - Barney's New York

107 **GLASSES** *(left to right)* - Persol; Giorgio Armani; Colors in Optic; **SUNGLASSES** - Ray-Ban

ACTIVE

110 **WHITE TANK** - Nike

113 **BLACK TOP & PANTS** - Patagonia

114–15 **JACKET & PANTS** - Eastern Mountain Sports; **HOODED JACKET & PANTS** - Moonstone

117 **RUNNING SHOES** - New Balance; **SOCKS** - Thor-Lo

118–19 **LOW-TECH SHOE** - Sperry Top-Sider; **HIGH-TECH SHOE** - Nike

120–21 **HOODED SWEATSHIRT** - Champion; **LEOTARD & LEGGINGS** - Reebok; **SPORTS BRA** - Jogbra; **RUNNING SHORTS** - Reebok; **DOUBLE-LAYER SHORTS** - Reebok; **AEROBIC SHOE** - Reebok

123 **GLOVES** - Good Hands; **HAT** - Olympian; **JACKET** - Hyde Park; **WHITE SHIRT** - Hyde Park; **JODHPURS** - Equestrian; **DRESS BOOTS** - Imperial

124–25 **QUILTED JACKET** - Barbour; **FLANNEL SHIRT** - Timberland; **LEATHER RIDING GLOVES** - Good Hands; **PADDOCK BOOTS** - Imperial; **RIDING JEANS** - Miller's Harness; **WESTERN BOOTS** - Dan Post; **RANCHER'S HAT** - Resistal

126–27 **TENNIS SKIRT** - Le Coq Sportif; **TENNIS SHOES** - Reebok; **SWEATER, POLO-SHIRT, SHORTS, JACKET & SOCKS** - Fred Perry; **GOLF SHOES & GLOVES** - Foot Joy

128–29 **FULL SUIT** - Body Glove; **SPLIT-TOE BOOTS** - O'Neil; **SURF TRUNKS** - Patagonia; **TANK SUIT** - Raisins; **GLOVES** - O'Neil; **SWIMSUIT & GOGGLES** - Speedo; **TOP & SHORTS** - O'Neil; **AQUA SHOES** - Nike

130–31 **BOOTS** - (left) Solomon, (right) Technica

132–33 **RIVER SANDAL** - Teva; **PADDLING PANTS & JACKET** - Patagonia; **HIGH BIB PANTS & JACKET** - High Seas; **¾ FINGER GLOVES** - High Seas; **OFFSHORE YACHTING BOOTS** - High Seas

135 **HAT, SHIRT, SHORTS, FISHING VEST, BOAT SHOES, WADING SHOES** - Orvis; **BELT** - Eastern Mountain Sports

136–37 **CLIMBING TOP & PANTS** - Black Diamond; **SHOES** - Scarpa; **CYCLING JERSEY, GLOVES, SHORTS** - Descente; **HELMET & SHOES** - Performance; **SOCKS** - Thor-Lo

139 **GLOVES** - Gates Gloves; **EARWARMERS** - Wig-wam; **SKI PARKA, PANTS, JUMPSUIT & BLACK ZIP TOP** - Bogner; **WHITE TOP** - Duofold; **GOGGLES** - Smiths

140–41 **HAT** - Wigwam; **EARWARMERS, GLOVES, ANORAK, WINDPANTS, ZIPPERED TURTLENECK, FLEECE VEST, GAITERS, TIGHTS** - L. L. Bean

MIXING

145 **WHITE SHIRT** - Polo/Ralph Lauren; **LEATHER JACKET** - Agnès B; **JEANS** - Levis; **T-SHIRT** - The Gap; **SUIT JACKET, PANTS, SKIRT** - DK Essentials; **CARDIGAN SWEATER** - Banana Republic

146–47 (*Attitude Adjustment*) **SUIT** - DK Essentials; **T-SHIRT** - The Gap; **SHOES** - Robert Clergerie; **BELT** - Polo/Ralph Lauren; **PRADA BAG** - Barney's New York. (*Bare Nights*) **SUIT SKIRT** & **JACKET** - DK Essentials; **LIME BAG** -

Ferragamo; **CHANEL SHOES** - Barney's New York; **JEWELRY** - Robert Lee Morris. (*Opposites Attract*) **JACKET** - DK Essentials; **JEANS** - Levis; **CARDIGAN SWEATER** - Banana Republic; **WHITE SHIRT** - Polo/Ralph Lauren; **SCARF** - Hermès; **PRADA KNAP SACK** - Barney's New York; **SHOES** - Keds; **PENDANT** - Robert Lee Morris. (*Mood Swing*) **WHITE SHIRT** - Polo/Ralph Lauren; **LEATHER JACKET** - Agnes B.; **SUIT SKIRT** - DK Essentials; **CHANEL SHOES** - Barney's New York; **JEWELRY** - Robert Lee Morris. - (*Personal Stamp*) **WHITE SHIRT** Polo/Ralph Lauren; **SUIT PANTS** - DK Essentials; **SCARF** - Hermès; **SHOES** - Robert Clergerie

148–49 (*Country Squire*) **QUILTED JACKET** - Barbour; **YELLOW JACKET** - Barney's New York Collection; **CHARCOAL VEST** - Barney's New York Collection; **WHITE SHIRT** - Polo/Ralph Lauren; **BLACK SKI PANTS** - Bogner; **BLACK RIDING BOOTS** - Imperial; **PLAID HAT** - Woolrich; **GLOVES** - Good Hands. (*Riding Habit*) **WHITE SHIRT** - Polo/Ralph Lauren; **SCARF** - Gucci; **KHAKI JODHPURS** - Equestrian; **BELT, LOAFERS, BAG** - Gucci. (*Fringe Element*) **RED FRINGE JACKET** - Polo/Ralph Lauren; **TAN VEST** - Barney's New York Collection; **WHITE SHIRT** - Polo/Ralph Lauren; **WHITE JEANS** - Polo/Ralph Lauren; **BROWN BOOTS** - Gucci; **GLOVES** - Good Hands. (*Scarf as Skirt*) **BLACK TANK** - Danskin; **SCARF** - Gucci; **SHOES** - Manolo Blahnik; **JEWELRY** - Robert Lee Morris

150–51 (*Horsey Set*) **RED SWEATER SET** - TSE Cashmere; **KHAKI JODHPURS** - Equestrian; **SCARF** - Gucci; **BELT** - Gucci; **BLACK BOOTS** - Robert Clergerie; **BRACELET** - Gucci. (*Classic Combo*); **RED CASHMERE SWEATER SET** - TSE Cashmere; **GRAY FLANNEL TROUSERS** - Polo/Ralph Lauren; **PEARLS** - CIRO; **GRAY FLANNEL SHOES** - Chanel; **BELT** - Gucci. (*High Cashmere*) **RED CASHMERE SWEATER SET** - TSE Cashmere; **SKIRT** - DKNY; **SHOES** - Donna Karan; **PEARLS** - CIRO

155 **NAVY JACKET & PANTS, VEST, KHAKIS** - Polo/Ralph Lauren

156–57 (*The Business Suit*) **SHOES** - Brooks Brothers; everything else from Polo/Ralph Lauren. (*Ivy League*) **JACKET** - Polo/Ralph Lauren; **STRIPED SHIRT** - Brooks Brothers; **SWEATER VEST** - Bergdorf Goodman Men; **JEANS** - Levis; **SATCHEL** - Coach; **LOAFERS** - Brooks Brothers. (*The Anti-Suit*) **VEST** - Polo/Ralph Lauren; **DENIM SHIRT** - The Gap; **KHAKIS** - Polo/Ralph Lauren; **KNAPSACK** - Coach; **LOAFERS** - Brooks Brothers. (*Off-Duty*) **SUIT** - Polo/Ralph Lauren; **SMEDLEY POLO SHIRT** - Bergdorf Goodman Men; **WATCH** - Timex; **SHOES** - Brooks Brothers

158–59 **BLACK CASHMERE CARDIGAN** - N. Peal. *(Classic Mix)* **CASHMERE CARDIGAN** - N. Peal; **GRAY FLANNELS** - Falke; **WHITE SHIRT** - Polo/Ralph Lauren; **BLACK SILK TIE** - Donna Karan Men; **SHOES** - J. M. Weston. *(Cashmere Casual)* **CASHMERE CARDIGAN** - N. Peal; **TURTLENECK** - Brooks Brothers; **SWEATPANTS** - Donna Karan Men; **DRIVING SHOES** - J. P. Todd. *(Paired with Plaid)* **CASHMERE CARDIGAN** - N. Peal; **DENIM SHIRT** - The Gap; **PLAID TROUSERS** - Brooks Brothers; **WATCH** - Sector; **LOAFERS** - Brooks Brothers. *(Formal Ease)* **CASHMERE CARDIGAN** - N. Peal; **SILK SHIRT** - Joseph Abboud; **FORMAL TROUSERS** - Joseph Abboud; **SUSPENDERS** - Cole Haan; **FORMAL SLIPPERS** - Edward Green; **WATCH** - Cartier; **SOCKS** - Barney's New York. *(Jazz Quartet)* **CASHMERE CARDIGAN** - N. Peal; **LEATHER JACKET** - New Republic; **JEANS** - Levi's; **HAT** - Worth & Worth; **WHITE SHIRT** - Polo/Ralph Lauren

FAMILY

162 **SNEAKERS** - Converse

164–65 **OVERALLS** - OshKosh B'Gosh; **BUGS BUNNY PAJAMAS** - J. C. Penney; **BATMAN PAJAMAS** - Kiddie City

173 **BLAZER, TIE, STRIPED SHIRT** - Brooks Brothers

QUOTES

Quotations not acquired directly through an interview were drawn from the following sources:

BASICS

2 **HENRY DAVID THOREAU**: *Walden and Other Writings of Henry David Thoreau* (New York: Modern Library, 1992)

34 **DIANA VREELAND**: *Clothes and the Man: The Principles of Fine Men's Dress* by Alan Flusser (New York: Villard Books, 1986)

36–37 **GEORGE FRAZIER**: Ibid.

40–41 **GIORGIO ARMANI**: American *Vogue*

50 **DONNA KARAN**: American *Vogue*

54 **HUBERT DE GIVENCHY**: comment made in 1952, reprinted in British *Vogue*

58 **COCO CHANEL**: *Chanel Solitaire* by Claude Baillén (London: William Collins & Sons Co. Ltd, 1973)

STYLE

76 **MICKY DREXLER**: *The New York Times*, August 23, 1992

OPTIONS

80 **SHERLOCK HOLMES**: as quoted in *A Gentleman's Wardrobe: Classic Clothes and the Modern Man* by Paul Keers (New York: Harmony Books/Crown, 1988)

88–89 **COCO CHANEL**: *Chanel* by Jean Leymarie (Geneva: Editions d'Arts Albert Skira, 1987). *Chanel Solitaire* by Claude Baillén (London: William Collins & Sons Co. Ltd, 1973). *Chanel: A Woman of Her Own* by Alex Madsen (New York: Henry Holt & Co., 1990). *Coco: The Life and Loves of Gabrielle Chanel* by Frances Kennett (London: Victor Gollancz Ltd.,1989)

105 **JACK KEROUAC**: *Dharma Bums* (New York: Viking Press, 1958)

107 "The Future's So Bright, I Gotta Wear Shades," by **PAT MACDONALD**, songwriter, published by Mamdadadi Music/I. R. S. Music (BMI), 1986

ACTIVE

120–21 **YVON CHOUINARD**: *Sport Illustrated*, February 11, 1991

130–31 **GANDHI**: as quoted in *The New Complete Walker* by Colin Fletcher (New York: Alfred A. Knopf, 1974)

134 **NORMAN MACLEAN**: *A River Runs Through It* (Chicago: University of Chicago Press, 1976)

MIXING

144–45 **DONNA KARAN**: *Women's Wear Daily*

147 **GEORGE BERNARD SHAW**, *Man and Superman* (1903)

147 **LAUREN HUTTON**: *Women's Wear Daily*

152–53 **DONNA KARAN**: American *Vogue*, August 1992

155 **MICHAEL KORS**: DNR

FAMILY

162 **FRAN LEBOWITZ**, *Social Studies* (New Random House, 1981)

166–67 **AGNÈS B.**: *Architectural Digest*, September 1989

168 **DR. EUGENE V. BERESIN**, director of training in child and adolescent psychiatry at Massachusetts General Hospital: in *The New York Times*, July 30, 1992

169 **JANE SMILEY**: *A Thousand Acres* (New York: Alfred A. Knopf, 1991)

173 **STEVE MARTIN**: in *The New York Times Magazine: Men's Fashions of the Times*, September 1988

PHOTO RESEARCH

FOUNDATION: (page 14, clockwise from top left) UPI/Bettmann; Burke Uzzle; UPI/Bettmann; Ron Galella; UPI/Bettmann; Archive Photos; Kobal Collection; Bettmann/Hulton; Reuters/Bettmann; Kobal Collection; Kobal Collection. **JEANS:** (page 58) UPI/Bettmann; (page 59, left to right) courtesy Levi Strauss & Co.; People Weekly © 1979 Evelyn Floret; Kobal Collection; © 1992 The Warhol Foundation for the Visual Arts, Inc. **BLACK DRESS**: (page 60) Bettmann/Hulton. **TRENCH:** (page 65, top to bottom) Springer/Bettmann; Springer/Bettmann; UPI/Bettmann; The Bettmann Archive. **VEST:** (page 87, top to bottom) Photofest; Kobal Collection; Globe Photos, Inc.; Kobal Collection. **JACKETS:** (page 92, left to right) Springer/Bettmann; The Bettmann Archive. **PEARLS:** (page 96) UPI/Bettmann

DESIGNER SPREADS

GIORGIO ARMANI: (page 40) Photo by Aldo Fallai, Fall-Winter 1977, courtesy of Giorgio Armani Uomo; **ZORAN:** (page 52) Photo by Ralph Dominguez, courtesy of Globe Photos, Inc.; **GEOFFREY BEENE:** (page 70) Photo courtesy of Jack Deutsch; **COCO CHANEL:** (page 88) Daniel Jouanneau; **DONNA KARAN:** (page 152) Courtesy of Donna Karan

Photo Research by **JANE D. MARSCHING**

ACKNOWLEDGMENTS

Barney's New York, Susan C. Burch, Tony Chirico, Lauri Del Commune, Dina Dell'Arciprete, Jane Friedman, Joanne Harrison, Patrick Higgins, Katherine Hourigan, Kurt Houser, Andy Hughes, Lesleigh Irish, Carol Janeway, Ruth La Ferla, Karen Leh, Anne McCormick, Sonny Mehta, Miranda Ng, Hellyn Sher, Ethan M. Sound, Anne-Lise Spitzer, Meg Stebbins, Robin Swados, Robert Valentine, Shelley Wanger, Charles W. Weiss, Esq.

CHIC SIMPLE STAFF

PARTNERS Kim & Jeff
ART DIRECTOR Wayne Wolf
COPY EDITOR Borden Elniff
STAFF Elizabeth Benator, Alicia Cheng, Vered Frank, Will Georgantas, Joanne Harrison, Babs Lefrak, Gillian Oppenheim, Victoria Rowan, Diane Shaw, Takuyo Takahashi

COMMUNICATIONS

Chic Simple is all about the timely communication of information to help make sense of the things around you—and it wouldn't be called "communication" if it weren't two-way. Your words of suggestion, praise, and even menace are very important to us and our goal of producing the smartest, most useful books we can. Please keep them coming. In your letters, many of you are curious about our other titles, so we've created a catalog, which you can receive by mailing us the shirt off your back, or just your address, to:

CHIC SIMPLE
84 WOOSTER STREET, NEW YORK, NY 10012
Fax: **(212) 343-9678**
Compuserve number: **72704,2346**
e-mail address: **info@chicsimple.com**
web site address: **http://www.chicsimple.com**

Stay in touch because . . .
"The more you know, the less you need."

Please let us know if you're interested in Chic Simple clothing patterns.

A NOTE ON THE TYPE

The text of this book was set in two typefaces: New Baskerville and Futura. The ITC version of **NEW BASKERVILLE** is called Baskerville, which itself is a facsimile reproduction of types cast from molds made by John Baskerville (1706–1775) from his designs. Baskerville's original face was one of the forerunners of the type style known to printers as the "modern face"—a "modern" of the period A.D. 1800. **FUTURA** was produced in 1928 by Paul Renner (1878–1956), former director of the Munich School of Design, for the Bauer Type Foundry. Futura is simple in design and wonderfully restful to read. It has been widely used in advertising because of its even, modern appearance in mass and its harmony with a great variety of other modern types.

DESIGNED AND COMPOSED BY
The Valentine Group
New York, New York

SEPARATION AND FILM PREPARATION BY
NEC, Inc.,
Nashville, Tennessee

PRINTED AND BOUND IN GREAT BRITAIN BY
Butler & Tanner, Ltd.
Frome and London

HARDWARE

Apple Macintosh Power PC 8100, Quadra 800 personal computers; APS Technologies Syquest Drives; MicroNet DAT Drive; SuperMac 21" Color Monitor; Radius PrecisionColor Display/20; Radius 24X series Video Board; Hewlett-Packard LaserJet 4, Supra Fax Modem.

SOFTWARE

QuarkXPress 3.3, Adobe Photoshop 2.5.1, Microsoft Word 5.1, FileMaker Pro 2.0, Adobe Illustrator 5.0.1.

MUSICWARE

Beck (*Odelay*), John Coltrane (*Newport '63*), The Crow: City of Angels (*Motion Picture Soundtrack*), Kenny Dorham (*Whistle Stop*), Bill Evans (*Moonbeams*), The High Llamas (*Gideon Gaye*), Jewel (*Pieces of You*), Jackie McLean (*New Soil*), Liz Phair (*Exile in Guyville*), Poe (*Hello*), Sonny Rollins (*Saxophone Colossus*), The Ska-talites (*Ska Authentic*), Phoebe Snow (*Greatest Hits*), Bruce Springsteen (*The Wild, the Innocent, and the E Street Shuffle*), George Strait (*Greatest Hits Volume II*), Toots & the Maytals (*Funky Kingston*), Traffic (*The Low Spark of High-Heeled Boys*), Trainspotting (*Motion Picture Soundtrack*).

"Until now, life, this simple thing, has not been properly seen. One did not know that it was so simple and clear, that one merely needed to organize it and free it from all excess. To work for life, not for palaces or temples, cemeteries or museums."

ALEKSANDR RODCENKO 1921